THE SOUTHERN KING ARTHUR FAMILY

Engine No 30768 Sir *Balin* at Bromley South with the Author on the footplate with Driver Gingell and Fireman Rowe.

THE
SOUTHERN
KING ARTHUR
FAMILY

O. S. NOCK, BSc, CEng, FICE, FIMechE

DAVID & CHARLES

NEWTON ABBOT   LONDON

NORTH POMFRET (VT)   VANCOUVER

ISBN 0 7153 7156 8
Library of Congress Catalog Card Number 76-2885

From the footplate of a King Arthur approaching Rochester Bridge Junction.

Set in 10 on 11 Baskerville
and printed in Great Britain
by Biddles Ltd, Guildford, Surrey
for David & Charles (Publishers) Limited
Brunel House Newton Abbot Devon

Published in the United States of America
by David & Charles Inc
North Pomfret Vermont 05053 USA

Published in Canada
by Douglas David & Charles Limited
1875 Welch Street North Vancouver BC

CONTENTS

ACKNOWLEDGEMENTS

The author and publisher wish to thank the following for permission to use photographs: British Railways, pp 9, 10, 13 top, 20, 21 top, 70, 72; R. Brookman, 65; E. D. Bruton, 76, 77, 78 top, 87 bottom; H. C. Casserley, 8, 14, 21 bottom, 26 top, 50 bottom, 51 bottom, 52, 59 top, 60 top, 61 bottom, 64, 67; John G. Click, 2, 4, 86; C. R. L. Coles, 69, 79; Derek Cross, 82, 83 bottom, 84 top, 85, 87 top; M. W. Earley, 37 bottom, 53, 57 top, 58 top, 59 bottom, 62, 71, 75; the late C. Laundy (courtesy of K. H. Leech), 39; K. H. Leech, 81; O. S. Nock, 17, 56, 58 bottom, 66, 68, 78 bottom, 83 top; North British Locomotive Company, 40-1; Ian S. Pearsall, 84 bottom; Dr P. Ransome-Wallis, 36 top, 36 centre; R. C. Riley, 80; Real Photographs Ltd, 7, 16, 19, 24 bottom, 27, 28, 29, 36 bottom, 37 top, 42, 46, 47, 48, 49.

The remainder are from the author's collection from the late W. J. Reynolds and the late F. E. Mackay.

PREFACE

It was once quite characteristic of a change of locomotive superintendents on the old railway companies of Great Britain that the new man took one look at the existing locomotive stock and then proceeded to design something entirely different. In the broadest sense this could have succinctly described what happened on the London & South Western Railway after the death of Dugald Drummond. The only thing was that Robert Urie did not need to take a look. As works manager at Eastleigh he knew the situation only too well. The later years of Dugald Drummond's career provide one of the greatest mysteries in British locomotive history, as to why, when his early work on the North British and on the Caledonian had been so outstanding, he could have become enmeshed in all the complications of great, but ineffective four-cylinder 4-6-0s. Many writers have made guesses at the reasons — some, one fears, in seeking more dramatic effect than engineering fact and reasoning. But whatever the underlying reasons may have been, Robert Urie went through

Drummond's practice, in its more fanciful excesses, like a tornado.

The first new engine, the H15 4-6-0 of 1913, represented one of the most significant departures from contemporary British practice that had been seen for many years, in the utter simplicity of its machinery. It found no great favour elsewhere for many years afterwards, or during the investigations of the Bridge Stress Committee in the 1920s. It was indeed only because the newly formed Southern Railway was in very urgent need of more powerful passenger engines that Maunsell and his staff took the Urie N15 as a quick expedient, because there was not time to design the contemplated four-cylinder 4-6-0.

This book tells how the modified N15 became one of the great engines of British locomotive history, and was in its layout of machinery the precise forerunner of the range of British standard locomotives introduced by R. A. Riddles from 1951 onwards. The 'King Arthur family', as I have called this group of

The first Urie 4-6-0, No 486, in Southern Railway days.

locomotives, stems directly from Urie's drastic changes in 1913-4. Four out of the six varieties were pure Urie, and the differences in detail can be studied from the diagrams and tables of dimensions at the end of this book; but one of the curiosities never explained by some of the men who knew them best was that the original N15s, though poor steamers until the Maunsell modifications were such supremely fast runners, even though their valve gear differed in some important respects from that of the King Arthurs proper.

I was fortunate enough to enjoy the close personal friendship of the late H. Holcroft. He was a remarkable man. In him were combined the expert outlook and wealth of experience of the professional engineer, with the almost boyish enthusiasm of the amateur lover of locomotives. In addition to many personal discussions he wrote me a volume of letters; and although his vivid memory contained innumerable anecdotes of men as well as locomotives he never once spoke ill of any colleague, even of the difficult days after Maunsell's retirement, when the 'new broom' of chapter six brushed him, and Clayton too, on to one side! This book could not have been written in its present form without the help I received from him.

I am also indebted to the running officers of the Southern Railway (and later the Southern Region) for many opportunities of observing the King Arthur class engines at work. In pre-war days there was A. Cobb, and A. B. MacLeod, another tremendous enthusiast, who was then assistant at Waterloo. In later years I enjoyed the friendship of T. E. Chrimes, who was running superintendent of the Southern Region, and my later footplate journeyings were most whole-heartedly aided and abetted by R. H. N. Hardy, when he was assistant running superintendent at Stewarts Lane shed. For the photographic side of the story I am much indebted to H. C. Casserley, who for many years lived in a house backing on to the former London, Chatham & Dover main line, near Bromley, and recorded many notable events while it is a privilege to be able to include some photographs taken by that one-time doyen of railway photographers, the late F. E. Mackay, notably that of *Sir Gawain* on the 11 am boat express on page 37.

Silver Cedars,   O. S. NOCK
High Bannerdown,
Batheaston,
Bath.   July 1975

Up Atlantic Coast Express passing Oakley; engine No 782 *Sir Brian*.

CHAPTER ONE

URIE — EPOCH-MARKING CHANGES

Dugald Drummond died on 8 November 1912, following a serious accident on the footplate, which involved the amputation of one of his legs. He died in his 73rd year, as he had lived, with locomotives. He has been represented as a tyrant; an irrational experimenter, whose latest and largest engines were little short of failures. But while it is often the idiosyncrasies of a man's character that receive the greatest attention from the casual producer of potted biographies, to dwell upon these in the case of Dugald Drummond would be to miss much of the truly great features of his life's work. Two of these features have a direct bearing on the present theme. Perhaps his greatest work was the designing and commissioning of Eastleigh Works, and little less in significance, the smooth transfer of all manufacturing and repair facilities thence from Nine Elms. Even greater was the way he attracted round him a team, not only of first rate engineers, but of shop foremen, running foremen, and of top link drivers. One might have thought that many Glaswegians would have been mighty glad to see the 'tyrant' go, when he was appointed to succeed William Adams on the London & South Western Railway, in 1896; but many of them, of all grades, came south to serve under him, the most distinguished of whom was R. W. Urie, who had been chief draughtsman on the Caledonian at St Rollox, and later works manager.

Urie, who had been locomotive works manager at Nine Elms and then at Eastleigh, was appointed chief mechanical engineer in January 1913 when he was already 58 years of age. He was one of those splendid railwaymen of the pre-grouping era who had, through long experience, an all-round knowledge of loco-

motive design, construction, and working, but no less a pleasant and equable temperament, quite unlike the fiery and irrational nature of his predecessor's make-up. Urie was well enough aware of the difficulties in running and maintenance continuously experienced with the big Drummond four-cylinder 4-6-0 locomotives, and with further large engines needed, he embarked upon an entirely new course — one that not only broke new ground on the London & South Western Railway, but one that was eventually to form the keystone of the locomotive

R. W. Urie, Chief Mechanical Engineer, LSWR 1912-1922.

policy of the nationalised British Railways, as initiated in 1951.

In complete contrast to the complications of the Drummond four-cylinder front-end layout, with some engines having dissimilar valve gear for the inside and outside cylinders, Urie's engines had two cylinders only, with outside Walschaerts valve gear. So far as the machinery layout was concerned, he was anticipating R. E. L. Maunsell's oft-repeated dictum: 'Make everything get-at-able'. In the same style all of Drummond's gadgets, such as cross-water tubes in the firebox, feed water heaters, and steam dryers were discarded, and a simple straight-forward boiler substituted. A very welcome feature so far as the footplatemen were concerned was the sloping firegrate, providing good depth under the brick arch at the front end. The boiler barrel, 13ft 9in long, was the same length as that of the Drummond 'paddle-boats', but the latter had a shallow horizontal grate extending over both the middle and rear coupled axles, and this made them extremely awkward to fire. Urie set the boiler further back so that the grate did not need to come over the middle coupled axle.

Ten of the new 4-6-0s were built, and Urie immediately showed his hand by fitting eight with superheaters, and having two using saturated steam. To gain experience of the two most popular varieties of superheater then coming into use in Great Britain at the time four were fitted with the Schmidt apparatus, and four with the Robinson. The respective dimensions and heating surfaces are shown in the table below. In view of subsequent developments on both the LSWR and the Southern Railway, it might be questioned whether there was really a need to have so many variations in superheater design, with, for example, a well tried apparatus like the Schmidt available, and already, by 1913, in worldwide application; but superheaters were things over which locomotive engineers of that era could get distinctly hot under the collar. I well remember the London divisional engineer of the Great Western once exclaiming: 'They advertise the Robinson superheater as "a sound running job"; but it isn't. It's a main works job'. There was another side to it, apart from design and maintenance. Superheaters were then patented, proprietary articles, and royalties had to be paid for their use. So engineers with good drawing offices at their disposal, set about designing their own, and patenting them!

The first Urie 4-6-0: No 486, Class H15 with Robinson superheater, built Eastleigh December 1913.

The first batch of five, completed at Eastleigh between December 1913 and March 1914, consisted of three Robinsons and two Schmidts, the respective numbers being 486-488 and 482-483. The second batch came between April and July 1914, in this order 484 (Schmidt), 489 (Robinson), 485 (Schmidt) and the two satura-tors last, 490 and 491 in June and July 1914 respectively. Contemporary observers noted, not entirely with approval, the absence of splashers, and the exposure of all the running gear, while another departure from previous LSWR practice was the design of the tender with outside-framed bogies, in contrast to the Drummond inside-framed water cart tenders. The cylinders of both saturated and superheated varieties were the same, namely 21in diameter, by 28in stroke, but the saturated engines carried a higher boiler pressure of 200 lb/sq in. They had large-ported 11in diameter piston valves, and proved very free running engines in express passenger service, although originally designated mixed traffic.

CLASS H15 :   BOILER VARIATIONS

Heating surfaces in Sq ft

Engine Numbers	482-5	486-9	490-1
Type of Superheater	Schmidt	Robinson	None
Small Tubes	1252	1252	2025
Large Tubes	507	464	-
Firebox	167	167	167
Total Evaporative	1926	1883	2191
Superheater	360	333	-
Combined Total	2286	2216	-
Grate Area	30	30	30

The new engines were put into service on express passenger trains, and indicator trials were conducted on the 11.10am West of England express between Waterloo and Salis-bury. All the Drummond locomotives with 6ft 7in coupled wheels, 4-4-0 and 4-6-0 alike, were fast runners, but it was soon evident that the Urie engines despite their smaller wheels were every bit their equal. Before world war I the fastest booked run on the LSWR was something of a stunt; the 5.3pm up from Basingstoke stopped at Vauxhall, covering the 46.5 miles in 49min, with a load usually less than 300 tons, and as the line has a falling tendency throughout it was not a difficult job. The first run ever to be published with one of the new engines was on this train, and details are set out in the accompanying table. It is clear that the engine

L S W R   BASINGSTOKE - VAUXHALL
Load: 245 tons tare, 260 tons full
Loco: 2-cylinder 4-6-0 No 486 (Class H15)

Dist Miles		Sch min	Actual m s	Av Speed m p h
0.00	BASINGSTOKE	0	0 00	-
5.61	Hook		7 30	44.9
7.89	Winchfield		9 41	62.6
11.29	Fleet		12 42	67.6
14.59	Farnborough		15 42	66.0
15.89	Sturt Lane Junc		16 48	70.8
19.89	Brookwood		20 21	67.5
23.47	WOKING	25	23 16	73.6
26.15	Byfleet		25 23	76.2
28.71	Weybridge		27 34	70.2
30.89	Walton		29 22	72.7
34.49	Hampton Court Junc	35	32 42	64.9
35.89	Surbiton		33 58	66.8
38.06	Malden		36 05	61.3
40.57	Wimbledon		38 29	62.3
42.28	Earlsfield		40 08	62.1
43.89	CLAPHAM JUNC	45	41 52	55.5
46.53	VAUXHALL	49	45 34	-

Max Speed near Byfleet   78½ m p h

was considerably eased after Hampton Court Junction, or a considerably faster end to end time could have been made.

In view of the reversion from four to two cylinders at a time when the engineers of British railways building the largest and most powerful types were tending to adopt three or four cylinders, it is interesting to examine what could be called the mechanics of these engines. They were built in the true Drummond battleship tradition, with 1¼in thick plate frames, and weighed 81¼ tons without their tenders. The weights on the three driving axles were originally given as 20.1, 20.2, and 20.15 tons from front to rear though these would appear to have under-gone some modification later. The reciprocating parts were generously balanced, by heavy weights in the coupled wheels, and this, while making them smooth and comfortable engines to ride had a murderous effect upon the track, which was not brought to general notice until the researches of the Bridge Stress Committee from 1924 onwards. Then it was shown that the original H15, as the class was known, had one of the highest dynamic augments, or whole engine hammer blows of any British locomotive examined. At a speed of 77mph (6 rev per sec) the loading was:

	Hammer blow tons	Max combined tons
Whole engine	25.5	—
Axle	10.5	30.3
Wheel	6.2	16.1

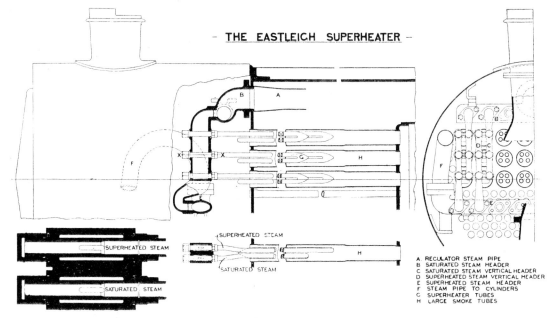

- THE EASTLEIGH SUPERHEATER -

SECTION AT X X   The 'Eastleigh' Superheater as designed by R. W. Urie.

Late in 1914 Urie brought out his own design of superheater, named the 'Eastleigh', and patented in his name. He described it thus:
'The saturated steam passes along pipe (A) from the regulator, when it is opened by the driver, into the upper saturated header (B), thence into the vertical distributing pipes (C), communicating with the header (B), when it passes to the interior of the tubes (G) through the slotted hole, shewn in enlarged section XX, returning to the vertical distributing pipes (D), communicating with the lower superheated header (E.).

'These tubes (G) are placed within large smoke tubes (H), traverse along to within about 2 feet from the firebox tube-plate, and are subjected to the high temperature gases from the firebox. They are each made up of four parts, with welded spear shaped connections at either end, forming an 'element', the steam has thus to pass four times through each element during which its temperature is raised. The number of elements used, and the nature of the work being done by the engine determines the temperature to which the steam is raised. The greatest number used on the L. & S. W. Rly. is 24, which gives a temperature of 650° Fah.

'The Steam when it leaves the regulator at 180 lbs per square inch working pressure has a temperature of 380° Fah, so that its temperature is raised to the extent of 270° Fah, but as already stated, without increasing its pressure, owing to the fact that the superheater, when in operation,

is in direct communication with the boiler and subject to the pressure determined by the safety valves.

'As the steam emerges from the tube (G), it passes through slot holes into the vertical distributing pipe (D), and thence down into the superheater header (E) as already stated above. From each end of (E) it is taken by a pipe (F) to the cylinders.

'As the distributing pipes (D & C) form a kind of screen in front of the tubes they act as a spark arrester, as the greater proportion of the sparks are drawn through the upper tubes.'

This description can be followed from the drawing reproduced on this page.

This arrangement successfully circumvented the Schmidt and Robinson patents, and it certainly proved very effective in service. It was first applied to an interesting addition to the H15 class. The last of the huge Drummond four-cylinder 4-6-0s of the 330 series, No 335 built in 1907 was different from the rest in having considerably larger cylinders; but it was perhaps even less successful than the others, and in November 1914 Urie rebuilt it completely as a two-cylinder engine of the H15 class, and having the Eastleigh superheater, instead of the Drummond cross-water tubes in the firebox. The original boiler was retained, though of course completely retubed to provide the following variation in heating surfaces:

A. REGULATOR STEAM PIPE
B. SATURATED STEAM HEADER
C. SATURATED STEAM VERTICAL HEADER
D. SUPERHEATED STEAM VERTICAL HEADER
E. SUPERHEATED STEAM HEADER
F. STEAM PIPE TO CYLINDERS
G. SUPERHEATER TUBES
H. LARGE SMOKE TUBES

The first LSWR No 335: Drummond's 4-cylinder 4-6-0 of 1907.

4-6-0 ENGINE No 335

Date	1907	1914
Form	4-cylinder	2-cylinder
Heating surfaces sq ft		
Small tubes	2210	1252
Large tubes	—	464
Water tubes in firebox	357	—
Firebox	160	168
Superheater	—	308
Total	2727	2192

The grate area remained the same, at 31.5 sq ft, but the rearmost coupled axle was set back so that a sloping grate as on the original H15 engines could be accommodated. As built in 1907 No 335 had the coupled axles spaced equally at 6ft 8in, whereas in the H15, and in the Urie rebuild of No 335 the spacing was 6ft 3in and 7ft 6in. The boiler pressure remained at 175lb/sq in as on the original Drummond engine.

Once the Eastleigh superheater had proved its worth on No 335 Urie lost no time in rebuilding the T14 series of four-cylinder 4-6-0s, the Paddleboats, taking out the steam dryers and cross water tubes and substituting Eastleigh superheaters. With those ten engines rebuilt, and their performance enhanced there was less need for the mixed-traffic H15s in passenger traffic, particularly on the attenuated and decelerated services of the later war period; and the Urie engines took up the work for which they had originally been designed. They proved

Urie's rebuild of No 335 in 1914, as in Southern Railway days: the first engine to have the Eastleigh superheater.

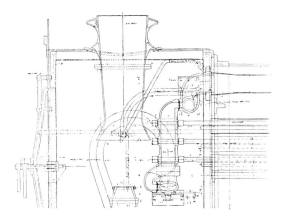
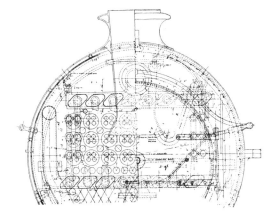

Smokebox arrangement, with Eastleigh superheater on rebuilt engine No 335.

singularly trouble-free engines, amassing large mileages with little in the way of week-to-week maintenance, and in the difficult conditions of wartime amply justifying the changes in basic design from previous LSWR practice made by Urie. It was no more than natural that a true express passenger version was considered, and in 1918 the first of the N15 class, with 6ft 7in coupled wheels, was completed at Eastleigh. While having all the basic characteristics of the H15 the new engines had an extra touch of austerity in the rather severe stove-pipe chimney.

The early records of the Urie H15s were rather remarkable. It is true that it was wartime, and engines were required to run longer mileages between general repairs than normally, but No 486, the first engine of the class ran for *seven years* before her first general overhaul. The following table gives the dates for the whole class. No 487 seems to have been a troublesome engine, while Nos 490 and 491 were brought in for superheating.

The N15 attracted attention on technical grounds from the use of cylinders no less than 22in diameter, but because of the larger coupled wheels the nominal tractive effort was roughly the same as that of the H15. There was a change in the boiler design. That of the H15 had two parallel rings, 5ft 7⅜in and 5ft 8¾in external diameter respectively, whereas on the N15 the forward ring was tapered, from 5ft 1⅜in diameter at the front to 5ft 4¾in at its junction with the second ring. This latter was 5ft 5¾in external diameter. The tube heating surfaces were the same as on H15 class, but both the firebox and superheater were less — 162 against 167 sq ft and 308 sq ft against 360 in the Schmidt superheaters of Nos 482 to 485. The slightly

Engine No.	Date first passed into traffic	Date called in for first general repair
482	14.3.14	13. 9.20
483	4.4.14	8. 7.20
484	23.5.14	5.12.19
485	10.6.14	6. 3.20
486	17.1.14	8. 3.21
487	21.2.14	19. 2.17
488	25.4.14	11.11.19
489	30.5.14	12.10.20
490	11.7.14	31. 5.19
491	31.7.14	14. 6.17

The first Urie H15 to have Schmidt superheater, No 482, on a special Bournemouth express passing New Malden.

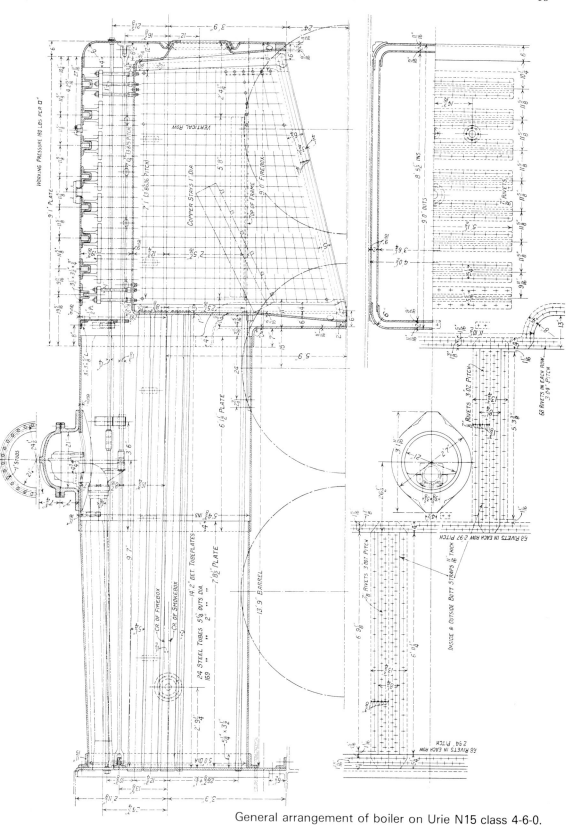

General arrangement of boiler on Urie N15 class 4-6-0.

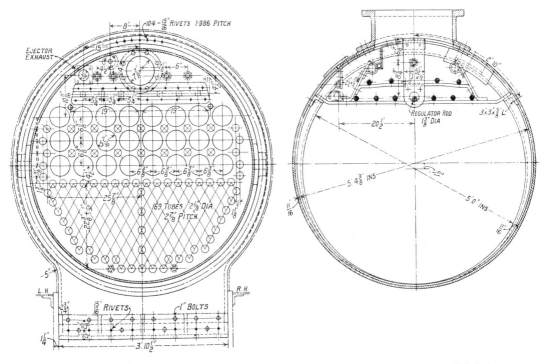

Cross sections of N15 boiler at front tube plate (left) and at the dome (right).

smaller boiler barrel had the effect of reducing the total engine weight in working order from 81¼ to 77¾ tons. Constructional details of the boiler can be studied from the drawing on page 15. The adhesion weight was reduced from 60.4 to 57 tons, though the N15 remained one of the most sure-footed of locomotive classes of which I have experience. The first three of the new engines, Nos 736, 737 and 738 were completed in 1918, and allocated to Nine Elms shed. The remaining seven came out at intervals between February and November 1919, and the

One of the first batch of N15 4-6-0s, introduced in 1918: No 740 afterwards named *Merlin*.

The second N15 to be built, No 737, shown beneath the great signal box that used to span all the tracks at Waterloo.

first to be stationed outside London was No 743, which was sent new to Salisbury.

In the technical press of the day, they had the most laudatory reception, though re-reading some of the reports today it does seem as though the praise given to them was rather fulsome, in view of the actual work they performed. They had their own regular drivers, and apparently no others, and in consequence the mileage run was exceedingly modest, amounting to about 35,000 per annum. In 1919 when the first detailed observations of their running was made by the late Cecil J. Allen, and others, the wartime maximum speed limit of 60mph was still in force, and the 10.50am West of England express out of Waterloo was allowed 103min to cover the 83.8 miles to Salisbury, non-stop, and 105min for the 75.8 miles on to Sidmouth Junction. On a run with the pioneer engine, No 736, on which the 50.4 miles from Waterloo to Worting Junction was covered in 63¾min just inside schedule, the regulator was full open through-out, and cut-off 35 per cent. This was with a load of no more than 350 tons. Maximum speed on the level did not exceed 56mph. West of Salisbury cut-offs of 50 and 55 per cent, with full

regulator, were the normal order of the day, even on such modest schedules. Contemporary reports suggested that this was very economical working.

My own earliest experiences of these engines, entirely as a passenger, were on the Bournemouth line, but with the exception of the 6.35pm up the Nine Elms turns were on the semi-fast trains. A London engine, usually an N15, used to come down on the 9.30am from Waterloo, and return at mid-afternoon, but on the 6.35pm up, which was one of the trains accelerated in 1921 to a 2¼ hour run, inclusive of a stop at Southampton, engine No 740 made a reasonably good trip, with a load of 350 tons. We lost 1¼min on the initial booking of 37min to Southampton, but then made substantial amends by a good climb from Eastleigh to Litchfield tunnel, averaging 46.3mph over the 13.6 miles of 1 in 250 gradient from Shawford to the summit box. The usually fast run from Basingstoke to Wimbledon was interrupted by a signal check at Fleet, to 40mph, but we ran the 40.6 miles in 39¾min, with a sustained maximum speed of 72mph downhill past Woking. Net time for the 79.3 mile run up from

Up West of England express in Clapham cutting, hauled by N15 4-6-0 No 737 afterwards named *King Uther*.

Southampton was about 90min.

I think there must have been some pangs of conscience over the gentlemanly existence the N15s were enjoying, because in 1922, the locomotive workings were altered to enable one engine to work through between Waterloo and Exeter, with remanning at Salisbury, thus practically doubling the daily mileage of the Nine Elms engines, but the only details of running recorded at the time showed these engines in a very poor light. Although suggestions made at the time sought to put at least some of the blame on the footplate crews, it was subsequently revealed — many years later — that this was not the case. It is now known that in those early days the engines were frequently in trouble for steam. Furthermore, even when steaming adequately the performance was not commensurate with the nominal heating surfaces and tractive effort of these large engines. The need to use full regulator and 35 per cent cut-off to produce a little under 60mph on level track with a 350 ton load hardly suggested an efficient locomotive. In 1920-1, on the easy schedules of that time the average all-round coal consumption of the 10 N15 engines was between 35 and 40 lb/mile, though many of the trains they were working loaded to little more than 250 tons.

From published details of running No 739 was the black sheep of the class, putting up indifferent and erratic performance in her earliest days, and her reputation was not enhanced in 1921, when during the prolonged coal strike of that year she was equipped for oil burning, together with No 737. The apparatus used on these two engines was the Scarab. On the 11am down West of England express, with a load of 365 tons, No 739 took 59¾min to pass Basingstoke, 80¼min to Andover, 66.7 miles, and 99½min to Salisbury, arriving there 4½min late on the accelerated schedule then in force. Until the summit beyond Battledown Junction was passed, the speed had not anywhere exceeded 57½mph, and on the steep downhill stretches beyond the maximum was only 72mph. Nevertheless, the LSWR appeared to be satisfied with these engines in general, and an order for another 10 was put in hand in 1922. The last two were not completed until after the grouping, but nevertheless bore the initials LSWR on their tenders like the rest of the class. While mentioning liveries, the 10 H15 engines were painted in the full passenger panoply of Drummond, with the elaborate lining, and multi-striped boiler bands. On the N15s Urie retained the brown borders on the tender and cab, but used the simple black and white lining elsewhere.

At the time of the grouping Urie was 68 years

One of the Urie S15 class 5ft 7in 4-6-0s, No 496, in Southern Railway style of painting.

of age. Whether he would have continued in office had there been no amalgamation one cannot say; but as things were his retirement was inevitable. Although later events confirmed that his N15 class were not all their most ardent supporters would have had us believe, they continued the philosophy of the two-cylinder 4-6-0, with outside Walschaerts valve gear, which will always be remembered as Urie's outstanding contribution to British locomotive history. His final addition to what I have called the King Arthur family came in 1920 in the S15

express goods 4-6-0. This was in every respect an N15 with 5ft 7in instead of 6ft 7in coupled wheels, except that the cylinders were 21in diameter instead of 22in, and, with the boiler set 4½in lower than on the express engines, a longer and still less prepossessing stove pipe chimney was fitted. There were 20 engines in this class dating from March 1920 to May 1921, and numbered 497 to 515, and 496 in order of building. The Urie contribution to the King Arthur family was thus 10 of Class H15; 20 of Class N15, and 20 of Class S15.

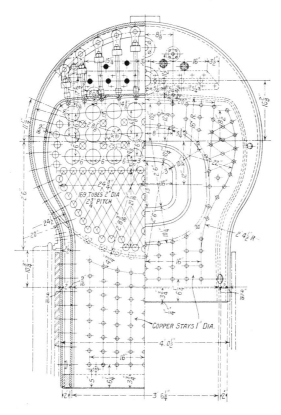

Cross section of firebox and back end view—boiler of N15.

CHAPTER TWO

URIE TO MAUNSELL

The amalgamations on 1 January 1923 produced no locomotive metamorphosis so clear cut as that on the Southern Railway. It was not only the top positions, but *every* key position that went to men of the former South Eastern & Chatham Railways Joint Managing Committee. That organisation was one of the very few in Great Britain that had adopted the Midland principle of having an independent officer responsible for locomotive running. On nearly all other railways the chief mechanical engineer had been responsible. The Southern adopted the SECR organisation in this respect, and R. E. L. Maunsell and A. D. Jones extended their previous responsibilities to cover the entire Southern Railway. For his own personal entourage at Waterloo, who became responsible for the initiation of all new designs, Maunsell picked none but ex-SECR men. The take-over was as complete as that of former LMS men, after nationalisation in 1948.

What proved to be the keystone of post-grouping locomotive practice on the Southern had been laid at Ashford in 1917 with the production of the prototype SECR six-coupled engines, the 2-6-0 No 810 and the 2-6-4 tank No 790. These, like the Urie H15, had two cylinders and outside Walschaerts valve gear, and J. Clayton, who had been chief locomotive draughtsman at the time and in SR days was Maunsell's personal assistant, freely acknowledged the benefit he derived from close association with G. J. Churchward of the Great Western. This had come about during the first world war when Maunsell was chief mechanical engineer to the Railway Executive Committee, and proposals were made for certain British standard designs for post war production. Churchward was one of the railway engineers who took much interest in this project, and Clayton had the job of working out the preliminary designs. It was then that he absorbed the Great Western precepts of boiler and valve gear design that were later turned to advantage on the Southern Railway. They had first been applied on the SECR prototype engines 790 and 810, and gave such encouraging results that they formed the basis of Clayton's further work after his move to Waterloo.

After the formation of the Southern Railway the newly appointed traffic manager, another

R. E. L. Maunsell: Chief Mechanical Engineer, Southern Railway, 1923-1937.

J. Clayton, Personal Assistant to the Chief Mechanical Engineer, from 1923.

SECR man, advised Maunsell that he would like to have locomotives capable of hauling 500-ton trains at start-to-stop average speeds of 55mph. It was clear that no existing locomotives of the LSWR or of the Brighton could remotely approach such a standard, while at the time of grouping the SECR had no passenger engines larger than the L class 4-4-0s. An entirely new design would have to be worked out. This would take time and consideration had to be given meanwhile to production of new locomotives in some urgency. Continental traffic was reviving rapidly, and civil engineering work was in hand to permit of the use of 4-6-0 locomotives on the boat trains to and from Victoria. Naturally the new locomotive management turned to the latest and largest of the pre-grouping express types, the LSWR N15 4-6-0, to assess its capabilities for wider use, as an interim expedient at any rate. Two things happened, and it is important to appreciate that they were no more than loosely connected. Clayton took the N15 design and modified it for future production, using his experience with the SECR N class 2-6-0, as a basis. Meanwhile, after Urie's retirement, any lingering delusions about the

success of the N15 vanished, and the running department who had to use the engines appealed to Maunsell to do something about their short-comings. The result was a series of investigations on engine No 742.

These tests, which took place in the spring and summer of 1924, have sometimes been thought to have been the preliminaries towards the design of the improved N15s, but actually the design of the modified N15, which emerged in 1925 as the King Arthur class, was complete in April 1924. The authority for the first 10 engines of the class, which became known later as the Eastleigh Arthurs, at first took the form of an order for rebuilding the 10 Drummond 4-cylinder 4-6-0s of the G14 class as two cylinder engines; but such was the need for high-speed express engines that the plan was revised to replace, rather than rebuild the 6ft engines, and have them still available in their original form for the summer traffic of 1924, when the motive power situation was expected to be critical. Taking events in chronological order there was first Clayton's redesign of the N15 front end. The boiler pressure was raised from 180 to 200 lb/sq in without alteration to the boiler design, but instead of the Eastleigh superheater Maunsell's own type, as designed at Ashford for the N class 2-6-0 was used. At the same time the cylinder diameter was reduced to $20\frac{1}{2}$ in. The piston valve diameter remained at 11in but the valve travel in full gear was increased from $5\frac{1}{8}$ in to $6\frac{9}{16}$ in. Much importance can be attached to this, but the design of the motion and the openings provided for steam and exhaust are in effect even more critical.

N15 class 4-6-0 No 742 fitted with indicator shelters for the first series of trials in 1924.

Another significant change was to provide increased air openings through the ashpan. The 10 new engines took the numbers and the tenders of the condemned G14s—namely 448 to 457.

There was also a change in the balancing, and while the King Arthurs were still rather heavy handed on the track, the hammer blow was reduced from that of the H15s as under:

	Hammer blow tons	Max combined load—tons
Whole engine	25.5	—
Axle	9.1	28.6
Wheel	7.3	17.1

The Maunsell superheater, features of which were patented in the names of Maunsell himself, and one of his earlier assistants at Ashford, Hutchinson by name, clearly reflects his aim to make every thing get-at-able. The first of the two

fixing bolts to pass through. The second drawing shows the patented arrangement for attaching the elements, with the ball-joint connections, to ensure steam tightness. The bolts were T-headed, adapted to pass through elongated slots in the flanges. In fastening they were turned through a right angle, and then rested in shallow retaining grooves. To remove an element all that was necessary was to slacken off the appropriate nut on the top of the header, turn the bolt through a right angle, and then lift it up clear through the elongated slot in the header. This form of superheater header was subsequently fitted to many ex-LSWR locomotives previously having the Eastleigh type, as well as to all new Southern Railway locomotives of Maunsell design.

Meanwhile, as drawings were being finished and work started at Eastleigh on the first 10 of the King Arthurs, the collateral project for

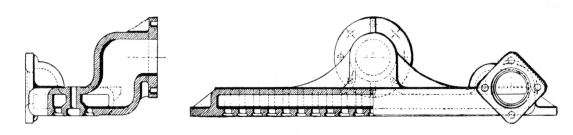

drawings reproduced shows how the saturated and superheated steam chambers were extended right across the header, with the dividing partition enlarged at intervals to allow for the

improving the Urie N15 class was getting under way. There is no doubt however that while using the latter as a basis for the new engines, Clayton did not altogether approve of the structural

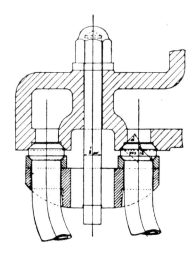

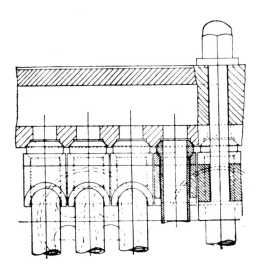

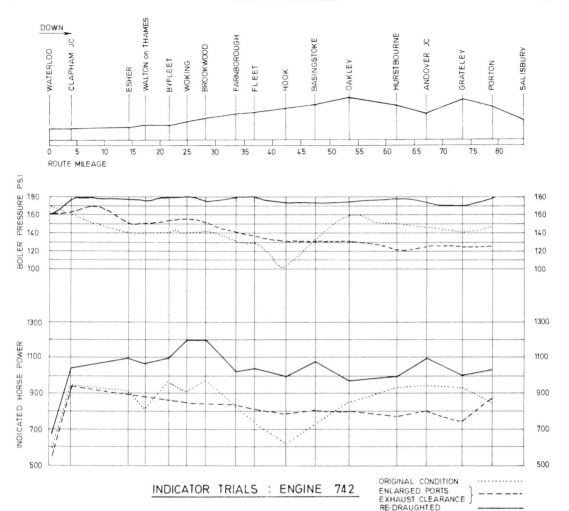

INDICATOR TRIALS : ENGINE 742

ORIGINAL CONDITION ....

ENLARGED PORTS }
EXHAUST CLEARANCE } — — — — —
RE-DRAUGHTED ————————

design, which he considered unduly ponderous, and asked Jock Finlayson, the old Scots chief draughtsman at Eastleigh how it was the Great Western could produce an engine with more than 30,000lb tractive effort for a total engine weight of 79¾ tons, whereas the Urie N15, weighing 77¾ tons had a tractive effort of only 26,200lb. All Clayton could get out of Jock was that he supposed 'the spec-ee-fic gr-r-ravity of steel was differ-r-rent at Swindon!' Moreover the first 10 King Arthurs came out at two tons heavier than the Urie N15s.

To return to the experiment with engine No 742, the first modifications included increasing the area of the steam and exhaust ports, and the provision of ⅛in exhaust clearance. The improvement was no more than marginal, with steaming remaining indifferent. Then the smokebox arrangements were completely changed, to include the draughting, blastpipe and chimney designed for the King Arthurs. It worked like a charm, and during the final series of tests the boiler pressure, in heavy steaming conditions, was maintained at 170 to 180 lb/sq in for 75 miles on end, with the indicated horsepower constantly over 1000 and sometimes rising to 1200.

An important point to be made at this stage is that the positive transformation that had been wrought in the performance of engine No 742 had not involved any change in the valve gear, which remained, as originally, with a maximum

The Urie N15 No 742 after draughting modifications, on 11 am West of England express: note modified chimney.

travel of 5⅛in and a steam lap of 1in. The immediate result of this development was that work could continue on the new engines with increased confidence in the efficacy of Clayton's front end arrangements while plans were made for bringing all the remaining Urie N15s into line with No 742. Nevertheless while these measures and the replacement of the 10 Drummond G14 4-6-0s by 10 new King Arthurs would go some way towards relieving the motive power situation on the former LSWR the all-line position was not so good. Design work was going ahead on the '500-ton-55mph' engines, but the first of these was not likely to be ready before the end of 1926, and if wholesale double-heading was not to be necessary on the Continental boat trains more powerful engines were urgently needed for the South-Eastern section. So the decision was taken to have 20 additional King Arthurs built by contractors. Drawings were available, patterns could be lent, but preparation of contract requirements took time, while one feature of the design itself needed changing. On the Eastleigh engines Nos 448-457 Finlayson had put the old LSWR type of cab, which had a profile that encroached upon the SECR loading

One of the earlier engines of the 1924 batch of H15 4-6-0s, No 476, having Eastleigh superheater: note absence of snifting valve on side of smokebox.

SECR N class 2-6-0 No 810, the design from which the draughting arrangements of the King Arthur class were derived.

gauge. So for the general service engines, for which a contract was placed with the North British Locomotive Company in December 1924, a cab like that of the SECR N class 2-6-0 was designed. Actually the order was for 30 engines, instead of the 20 originally projected.

To meet the general shortage of big engines on the Southern Railway a batch of 10 new H15 mixed-traffic 4-6-0s was built at Eastleigh in 1924. Except in one respect they were pure Urie, having chassis, wheels, and cylinders like the original H15s of 1913, but with the partially coned boiler of the N15 express engines. The 10 locomotives were numbered 473 to 478 and 521 to 524, and all except the last mentioned had Eastleigh superheaters. Engine No 524 was the first Southern 4-6-0 to have the Maunsell superheater. The new engines went into service between February and September 1924, and all originally had the Urie front end arrangements. They were all put into passenger traffic, Bournemouth shed getting its first 4-6-0s, while a few worked on the Portsmouth line. The only novel feature of their equipment was the use of a crosshead pump, in GWR style, for maintaining vacuum while running. Like the original H15s they were painted in the passenger engine colours. The tenders, while of the same general design as those of the N15 express engines were

S R   6.30 p m   WATERLOO-BOURNEMOUTH

Load: 11 coaches, 336 tons tare, 355 tons full

Engine: Class H15 4-6-0 No 523

Dist. Miles		Sch min	Actual m s	Speeds m p h
0.0	WATERLOO	0	0 00	–
–			sigs	
3.9	CLAPHAM JUNC	7	7 40	–
–			sigs	–
7.3	Wimbledon		13 40	–
–			sigs	
12.0	Surbiton		22 20	–
14.7	Esher		25 15	56
19.1	Weybridge		30 25	53/60½
24.4	WOKING	29	36 00	52
31.0	Milepost 31		44 30	42½
36.5	Fleet		50 50	57
39.7	Winchfield		54 15	54
42.2	Hook		57 05	60½
47.8	BASINGSTOKE	56	62 40	58
50.3	Worting Junc	59	65 35	44
58.1	Micheldever		75 50	61½
66.6	WINCHESTER		83 10	70
73.6	EASTLEIGH	83	89 30	–
78.1	Northam Junc	88½	94 35	–
79.2	SOUTHAMPTON	92	97 45	–
3.3	Totton	6½	6 30	–
6.1	Lyndhurst Road		10 45	53
8.8	Beaulieu Road		14 05	46
13.5	BROCKENHURST	18	19 10	61½
16.3	Sway		22 25	42
21.9	Hinton Admiral		28 15	65½
25.1	Christchurch		31 35	–
–			p w s	–
28.8	BOURNEMOUTH	36	39 35	–

Original form of the H15 class of 1924, generally the same as N15 but with smaller coupled wheels.

of slightly smaller capacity, holding 5000 instead of 5200 gallons of water.

As a traveller on the Bournemouth line at the time I had opportunities of observing the performance of these engines, and I was not at all impressed. In general the big Drummond D15 4-4-0s, with Eastleigh superheaters, could run the proverbial rings round them. The accompanying log overleaf on the 6.30pm down from Waterloo, which I recorded in the winter of 1924-5 is, within my own experience, typical. It is hardly possible to debit more than 5min to the string of checks encountered in the early stages, and then, after passing Woking 7min late only a

meagre 30sec had been recovered by the time Eastleigh was passed. Such minimum speeds as 53mph at Walton, 42½ at Milepost 31, 54 at Winchfield, and 44 at Battledown Junction were very poor for an engine of such nominal tractive power, while the running on the level was sluggish in the extreme. The work beyond Southampton was no better, with speeds as low as 46mph at Beaulieu Road, and 42mph up the Sway bank. The net times on the two stages of 92½ and 36½min were not flattering to the design.

A run with the last engine of the series, No 524 fitted with a Maunsell superheater was

The 1924 rebuild of the Drummond 330 class of 4-cylinder 4-6-0 of 1905, to be included in Class H15. The original boilers were used, but with Maunsell superheaters.

even less inspiring. With a load of only 315 tons the time from Bournemouth to Southampton was 38min, and although the train was running about 10min late the speed on the bank from Shawford up to Litchfield averaged no more than 46½mph, and speed at no time exceeded 65mph east of Basingstoke. The 64.6 miles from Southampton to Esher took 77¾min and then a succession of signal checks caused the last 14.7 miles into Waterloo to take 28¼min. I am afraid that by that time I did not look forward to my periodic journeys to Bournemouth with any great enthusiasm. I was not then in any position to ascertain the causes of such poor running, but from whatever cause it did not improve the rather tattered public image of the Southern Railway at that time. To all outward appearances it seemed that the H15s of this 1924 batch had all the failings of the N15s, with less capacity for speed because of their smaller coupled wheels.

The last production in the pre-Maunsell mould was the rebuilding of the five Drummond 4-cylinder 4-6-0s of the 330 class as 2-cylinder engines, in 1924-5. These engines were very extensively reconstructed, having the wheel spacing altered as well as the cylinder layout. But the original boilers were used, with the addition of Maunsell superheaters. Despite their shortcomings in service the original Drummond engines had a massive elegance in appearance, but this vanished in the rebuilds, when the enormous boiler was set above a straight, high-pitched running plate, and gave the engines a top-heavy look. I well remember my first sight of one of them, in 1925. I was in Exeter, and though my interests were then mostly concentrated on the GWR I did find time to go up to Queen Street, as it was then called, to have a look round. When No 332 arrived from

ATLANTIC COAST EXPRESS	:		SIDMOUTH JUNCTION-SALISBURY

Load: 13 coaches, 419 tons tare, 450 tons full

Engine: H15 4-6-0 No 333 (rebuilt Drummond)

Dist		Actual	Speeds
Miles		m s	m p h
0.0	SIDMOUTH JUNC	0 00	-
1.3	Milepost 158	3 13	45
4.6	Honiton	9 44	24½/26½
5.8	Milepost 153½	12 35	22½
11.5	SEATON JUNC	18 34	83½
14.8	Axminster	21 07	71
19.9	Chard Junc.	26 18	54
25.8	Milepost 133½	34 07	37½
27.9	Crewkerne	36 38	75
33.1	Milepost 126½	41 26	52
36.7	YEOVIL JUNC	45 03	69
41.3	Sherborne	49 28	57
43.9	Milepost 115½	53 15	28
47.4	TEMPLECOMBE	58 26	68 (max)
51.9	Milepost 107½	63 21	39½
54.2	Gillingham	66 05	54½
58.3	Semley	72 16	29½
67.6	Dinton	81 40	74 (max)
73.3	Wilton	86 56	-
75.8	SALISBURY	90 18	-

Salisbury with a down express I could scarcely believe my eyes! I had not then heard that any of them had been rebuilt.

I had an even greater surprise a few years later when I arrived at Exeter to catch the Atlantic Coast Express to Waterloo, and instead of the expected King Arthur found another of these rebuilt Drummonds waiting to take us as far as Salisbury. Although not up to King Arthur standard the engine put up a remarkably good show, as will be seen from the accompanying log. From Exeter the load was a fairly manageable one of 10 coaches, but this was increased to 13 from Sidmouth Junction, with a gross load of 450 tons. It was a tremendous proposition over so difficult a route, where loads much over 350 tons were something of a rarity in the 1920s. But the

One of the original series of H15s, in 1914 using saturated steam: here shown fitted with a stovepipe chimney.

The last of the 1924 batch of H15 4-6-0s No 524: first Southern engine to have the Maunsell superheater.

really surprising thing about this journey was the freedom with which this 6ft wheeled locomotive ran downhill. Such speeds as 83½mph down Seaton bank, 75mph at Crewkerne, and 67 to 74mph on the easier descent from Semley towards Wilton, were exceptional from any variety of the H15 class. The uphill speeds, with such a load as 450 tons, were as good as anything I have seen with an N15 before the Maunsell alterations; it must be recalled that the minimum speeds of 22½mph at Honiton Tunnel, 37½mph at milepost 133½, 28mph up Sherborne bank, and finally 29½mph at Semley came after appreciable lengths of ascent at 1 in 85-100, 120, 100-120, and 100. To average 50.3mph from start-to-stop was a highly creditable performance.

To conclude this note on working between Salisbury and Exeter, I have tabulated brief details of about the best run I have seen with an N15 engine in its original condition, on the summer schedule of the up Atlantic Coast Express, non-stop from Exeter to Salisbury, and allowed 102min for the 88-mile run. Passing Sidmouth Junction at speed engine No 745 got a better run at the steep final ascent to Honiton Tunnel, and from there the 70.0 miles to Salisbury took 76min 32sec against the 77min 43sec of my own run with No 333, carrying a heavier load.

So, with the rebuilding of the five 330 class Drummond engines the prelude was practically

EXETER-SALISBURY

Load: 12 coaches, 394 tons tare, 415 tons full

Engine: Urie Class N15 4-6-0 No 745

Dist		Actual		Speeds
Miles		m	s	m p h
0.0	EXETER	0	00	-
4.8	Broad Clyst	8	22	64½
8.5	Whimple	12	41	31½
12.2	SIDMOUTH JUNC	18	30	-
16.8	Honiton	25	15	-
18.0	Milepost 153½	27	38	29
-		p w s		-
23.7	SEATON JUNC	34	32	71½
32.1	Chard Junc	43	43	-
40.1	Crewkerne	54	20	40½/77½
48.9	YEOVIL JUNC	62	10	-
59.6	TEMPLECOMBE	74	52	32/75
66.4	Gillingham	81	25	-
70.5	Semley	86	31	37
79.8	Dinton	95	30	70½
88.0	SALISBURY	104	10	-

Net time 103 min

ended. Urie had done a great job in establishing the ultra-simple, get-at-able, 2-cylinder 4-6-0 with outside Walschaerts valve gear, but something seems to have gone adrift with the draughting arrangements between the original H15 engines and the N15s. Although contemporary observers and writers strove hard to put the best face possible on the locomotive situation on the South-Western section of the Southern it was undistinguished, and part of a prelude that gave little suggestion of the brilliant era that was so soon to follow.

CHAPTER THREE

INTRODUCTION OF THE KING ARTHURS

During the first years after grouping the Southern, in the eyes of the popular press of the day, could do nothing right. Every innovation, every attempt at rationalisation of train services as between hitherto competing routes was damned from the outset. 'Chaos on the Southern' was a frequent headline in the London papers. There were times when Sir Herbert Walker hit back, as when a deputation of season-ticket holders from Eastbourne protested about the state of the carriages, and got the curt reply that it was due to the filthy habits of the passengers! But by the autumn of 1924 things had gone far enough, and Sir Herbert Walker decided to pluck the nettle. The *Daily Express*

and the *Evening Standard* had been the spear-heads of the attack, and in January 1925 Walker appointed as his personal assistant, to take charge of publicity and advertising, a dynamic young journalist of 26, and who had already reached the height of Assistant Editor of the *Evening Standard*—John Blumenfeld Elliot. He was also related to the late Lord Beaverbrook. Never, in the history of railway public relations was there so dramatic a change as that which the Southern Railway came to enjoy.

So far as the present theme is concerned, the principal innovation was the introduction of systematic naming of express passenger loco-motives. Elliot was doubtless aware of the public

One of the first Eastleigh built King Arthurs of 1925, No 452 *Sir Meliagrance*, replacing the G14 four-cylinder 4-6-0 of the same number.

interest taken in Great Western locomotives, which had been intensified by the blaze of publicity surrounding the introduction of the Castle class 4-6-0s in 1923; but when he put the idea up to Sir Herbert Walker, the general manager told him to go and see Maunsell. The idea of naming the crack express locomotives of the Company after the Knights of the Round Table, and other personalities and places connected with the Arthurian legend was a stroke of genius, though when Elliot put the proposal to Maunsell, the mind of the CME was obviously running on different lines, for he replied: 'Tell Sir Herbert I have no objection, but I warn you it won't make any difference to the working of the engine!' And so the new 4-6-0s that were to replace the Drummond G14 class became the first of the King Arthur class. When engine No 453 was shown to the press and the public at Waterloo it was acclaimed as the harbinger of a new era on the Southern, though railway enthusiasts saw little different from the Urie N15 except the shape of the chimney, outside steam pipes, and the name.

The principal dimensions of the class were:

Boiler:

Diameter of barrel outside, max.	5ft 6in
Tubes, small: Number	167
Outside diameter	2in
Superheater flues: Number	24
Outside diameter	5¼in
Length between tube plates	14ft 2in

Heating surfaces:

Small tubes	1252 sq ft
Superheater flues	464 sq ft
Firebox	162 sq ft
Superheater elements	337 sq ft
Combined total	2215 sq ft
Grate Area	30 sq ft

Cylinders: Two

Diameter	20½in
Stroke	28in

Motion: Type — Walschaerts

Diameter of piston valves	10in
Max. travel of valves	6⁹⁄₁₆in
Steam lap	1½in
Exhaust Clearance	NIL
Lead	¼in
Cut-off in full gear	75%

Tractive effort:

At 85% working pressure	25,320 lb

Weights:

Total engine weight	80 tons 19 cwt
Adhesion weight	60 tons
Tender, loaded	57 tons 11 cwt
Coal capacity	5 tons
Water capacity	5000 gall

The first of the Scotchmen, No 763 *Sir Bors de Ganis*, at Stewarts Lane.

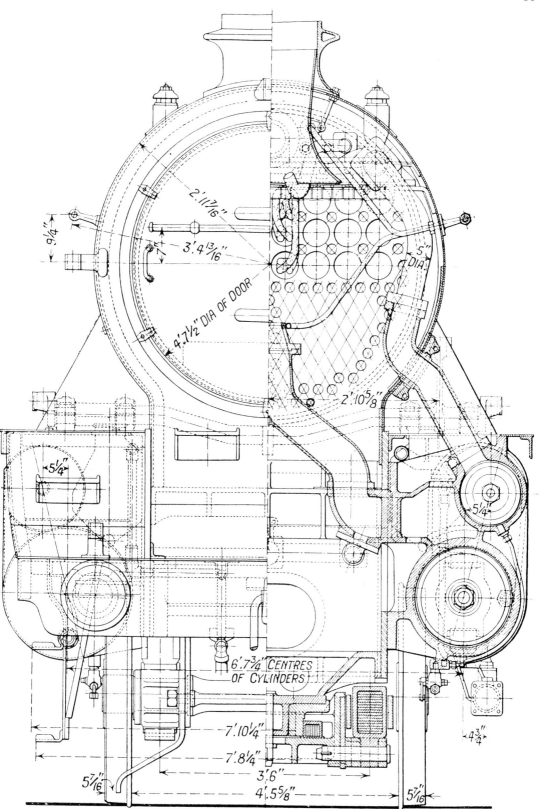

Front view drawing and section through cylinders, King Arthur class.

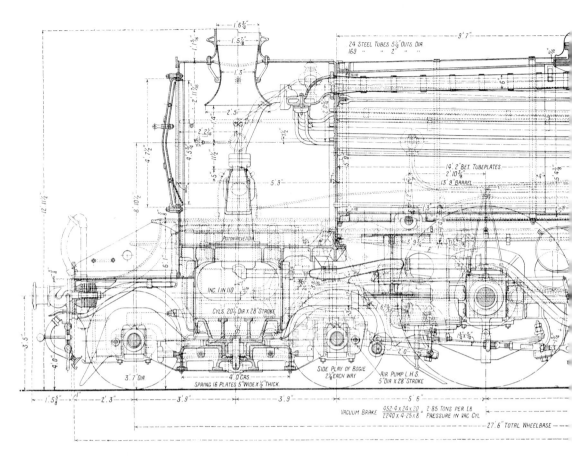

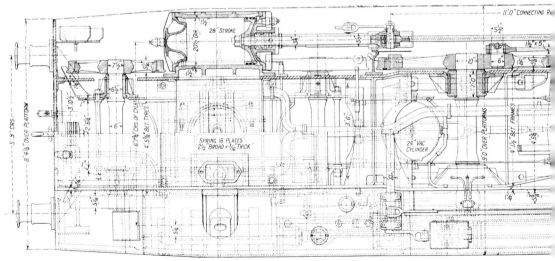

SECTIONAL ELEVATION AND PLAN OF "KING ARTHU

Mr. R. E. L. Maunsell, C.B.E., Chief Mechanical Eng

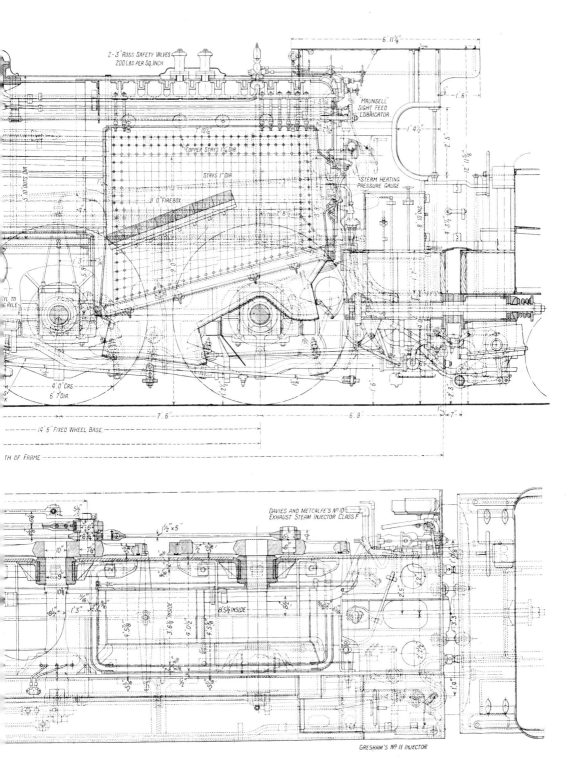

-0 TYPE LOCOMOTIVE, SOUTHERN RAILWAY.

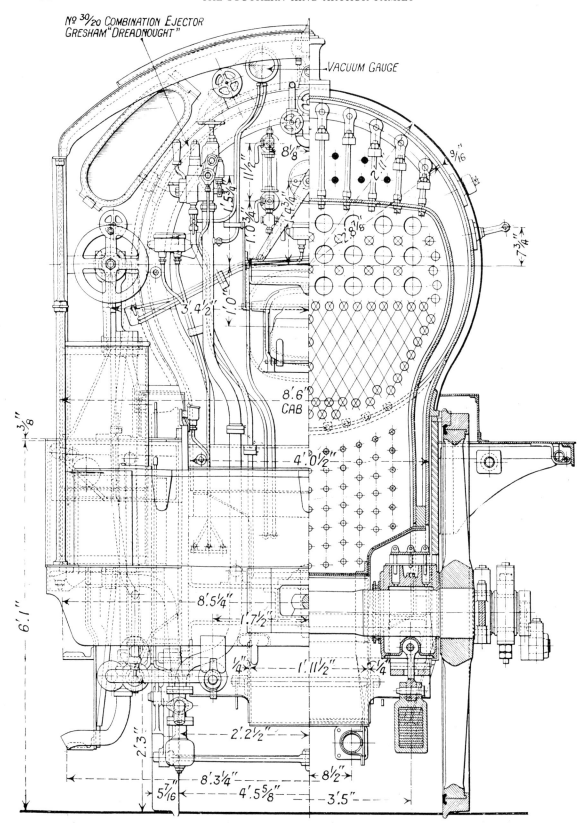

Cab view drawing and section through firebox.

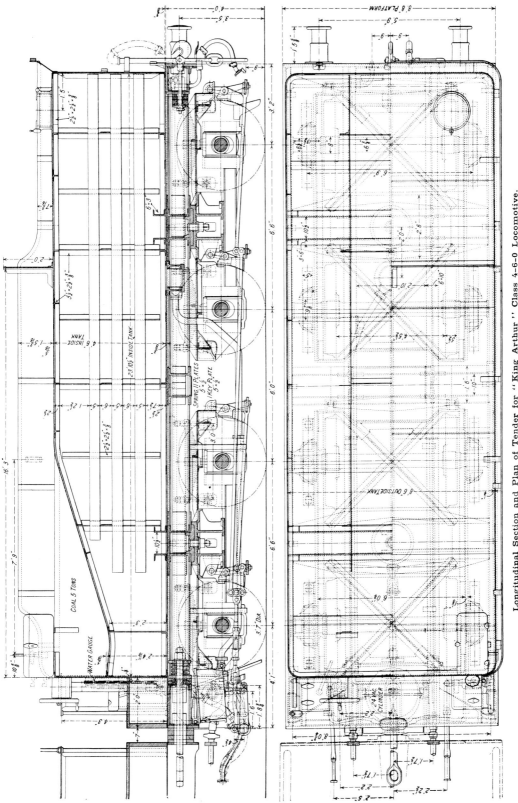

Longitudinal Section and Plan of Tender for "King Arthur" Class 4-6-0 Locomotive.

Two of the Scotchmen begin their journey southwards from Glasgow hauled by a North British Railway 0-6-0.

One of the Nine Elms Scotchmen No 775 *Sir Agravaine* on up West of England express in Clapham Cutting.

The 11 am Continental boat express, on the connecting line between Bickley and Orpington Junctions: engine No 764 *Sir Gawain.*

Engine No 787 *Sir Menadeuke* on up Bournemouth express near Basingstoke when much ex-LSWR rolling stock was still included in the train formations.

The practice of naming was extended to other locomotives besides the new 4-6-0s. The Urie N15s were incorporated in the King Arthur class, and received appropriate names, but as sometimes happens when systematised class naming is applied, the results can become faintly ridiculous, as when the Brighton Atlantics were named after headlands on the South Coast, and one of them was duly christened *Portland Bill!* With the King Arthurs it was perhaps inevitable that as the list lengthened so the names of the gallant knights became more and more unfamiliar, and some of the best known names were to be found among the first batch of ten, that replaced the G14s, and upon the Urie N15s. There were one or two curiosities among the names chosen. Among the Urie Arthurs for example, two engines were named after the same person, because *Elaine* (No 747) *was* the *Maid of Astolat* (No 744), while another beautiful name, bestowed on No 753, *Melisande* was that of a lady having no connection with the legend. Then it was originally intended to name one of the Glasgow engines *Sir Mordred*, till someone pointed out that as a dark traitor he was not exactly a desirable person to commemorate in a class otherwise representing the heights of early English chivalry. This engine thereafter took the road as *Sir Valence* and was the one that posed for the official photograph at the Hyde Park Works of the North British Locomotive Company.

In details of outward appearance the first of the new engines, No 453 *King Arthur*, completed at Eastleigh, was a synthesis of Maunsell, Urie and Drummond, having the cab of the original N15, the G14 tender, with inside frames, but the shapely Maunsell chimney gave the engine a much finer appearance than that of the Urie N15, and the direct outside steam pipes made the later engines distinguishable from their Urie predecessors, even after the latter had acquired the Maunsell type of chimney. It is interesting that when No 453 was first illustrated in *The Railway Magazine*, in May 1925, it was described as a rebuild. At the same time the full list of the 60 chosen names when published, included *Sir Modred* (sic), and the nickname *Sir Beaumains*, which was never actually used. The complete list is given at the end of this chapter. There was one other curiosity about the naming. In the lists published in two different railway journals at the time the name of No 451 was given as *Sir Llamorak*, but the engine never took the road with its name thus. The 40 new engines were put into traffic in 1925, by which time also

the 20 engines of the original Urie N15 class had been modified to agree with No 742, and had the new style of chimney. The G14 replacements, known as the Eastleigh Arthurs were mostly on the West of England main line, while of the new engines Nine Elms, Bournemouth and Stewarts Lane sheds received 10 each.

The numbers of the new engines built in Glasgow did not run consecutively from the Urie Arthurs 736-755. The numbers 756-762 remained blank, and the 'Scotchmen' as they were always known on the Southern, began at 763. The purists may tilt at this nickname, murmuring Scots, and Scottish under their breaths, but I am sorry to say that if one talked about 'Scotsmen' to anyone in the locomotive department of the Southern, if he did not look completely blank he would probably think you were talking about some alien type that went north from Kings Cross! Of the thirty Scotchmen Nos 763-772 went to Stewarts Lane for the Continental workings; 773-782 went to Nine Elms, and 783-792 to Bournemouth. The pioneer engine led a somewhat nomadic existence at the start, spending some months at Nine Elms, but later, the chivalrous monarch joined his queen at Salisbury. There was a report that engine No 453 worked the 1.6pm express from Charing Cross to Folkestone and Dover, though in the ordinary way the Eastleigh Arthurs with their Urie cabs were not allowed to work other

BOURNEMOUTH-WATERLOO : : : 2.35 p.m in JUNE 1925

Load: 13 coaches, 362 tons tare, 390 tons full

Engine: 4-6-0 No 453 King Arthur

Dist		Sch	Actual	Speeds
Miles			m s	m p h
0.0	BOURNEMOUTH	0	0 00	-
3.7	Christchurch		7 00	56
-			sigs	37
6.9	Hinton Admiral		12 00	40/30½
12.4	Sway		19 50	52½
15.2	Brockenhurst	20	22 45	65
22.6	Lyndhurst Road		30 00	60
25.4	Totton		32 50	64½ (max)
28.7	SOUTHAMPTON	37	37 30	-
5.7	EASTLEIGH	10	10 15	45
12.6	Winchester		19 55	42
14.7	Winchester Junc		22 45	45
21.1	Micheldever		31 15	43½
23.1	Litchfield Box		34 05	41½
28.9	Worting Junc		41 00	-
31.4	BASINGSTOKE	42	43 15	72½
37.0	Hook		48 05	61
42.8	Fleet		53 20	68
46.0	Farnborough		56 20	64½
48.3	Milepost 31		58 35	60
54.9	WOKING	64	64 40	69
60.2	Weybridge		69 05	71½/62
64.9	Esher		73 15	64½
67.2	Surbiton		75 45	61
72.0	Wimbledon		80 40	55
-			sigs	-
75.4	CLAPHAM JUNC	84	84 35	-
-			sigs	
79.3	WATERLOO	92	92 55	

than on former LSWR lines.

My own first experience of the class was also appropriately with engine No 453, on the 2.35 pm up 2¼ hour Bournemouth express, in the summer of 1925. Although the South-Western men had always been brought up to run with a full open regulator and the reverser wound well up they took a little time to get the feel of the new engines, and were inclined to pull them up a little too short on the lever. The work was leisurely to a degree. In respect of the valve gear it is important to emphasise that having long-lap, long travel valves, and a travel of 6⁵⁄₁₆ in in full gear they anticipated the famous locomotive interchange trials of 1925 between the Great Western Castle and the Gresley Pacific, which is sometimes quoted as the starting point for the introduction of modern valve gears in the Great Western style. When Maunsell crossed from Ireland to become chief mechanical engineer of the South Eastern & Chatham, in 1913, it was as a workshop man and a first-rate organiser rather than an engine designer that his reputation had been made. The design of the L class superheater 4-4-0s was in an advanced stage, but before placing contracts for their construction, Maunsell took the unusual step of sending the valve and valve gear design over to Inchicore for the opinion of his old chief draughtsman, W. Joynt, but by the time he had built up his new team at Ashford, Maunsell had every confidence in Clayton, who in turn had benefited enormously from his association with Churchward during the war. Clayton had already put long-travel valves on the prototype 2-6-0 and 2-6-4 tank, and using the Stephenson link motion on the rebuilt E1 and D1 4-4-0s.

An abbreviated log of my first run with a King Arthur is set out in the adjoining table. By later standards it was very dull, with a slow recovery from the slight signal check before Hinton Admiral, poor speed through the New Forest, and a restart from Southampton as though we had all the time in the world. The reasonably good speed from Basingstoke onwards was no doubt made under very easy steam. It was certainly better than my previous experiences with Urie 4-6-0s, but that is really all that could be said for it. Engine No 453 was a trial unit in several ways, and there may have been method

One of the Eastleigh six-wheeled tender batch of 1926-7 No 796 *Sir Dodinas le Savage* on the Southern Belle, near Purley.

North British Locomotive Company of
Valence, in photographic grey, showing

in the way it was being handled on this journey of mine. I had no conversation with the enginemen either before or after the run. As early as April 1925 a series of trials were made between Waterloo and Salisbury to compare the results of working with South Wales and Yorkshire coal, and to see if there was any appreciable difference in the coal consumption if Welsh coal was passed through a mechanical loading plant. The train in each case was the Atlantic Coast Express, made up to 12 coaches, and with the coaching stock then in use the tare load, on fifteen return trips, varied between 310 and 339 tons. Schedule time for the non-stop run

of 83¾ miles was 92min down, and 93min up. Coal consumption per engine mile varied between 35 and 42lb — the heaviest use being on the test when Welsh coal was taken from the mechanical loading plant.

Although these trials, which continued into June 1925 were primarily a comparison of coals they did show the new engines in a favourable light, not only so far as actual consumption was concerned but in free running and free steaming. My own run on the 2.35pm up from Bournemouth was made only a fortnight after the conclusion of the coal trials. While the locomotive testing section was carrying out

...tograph of a Scotchman No 767 *Sir*
...ls in great clarity.

indicator trials with engine No 451 *Sir Lamorak*.
Again the Atlantic Coast Express was chosen,
and the load specially augmented to 14 coaches,
a tare load of 440 tons. For 86min out of the
journey time of 93min the regulator was full
open, and 14 indicator cards taken between
Esher and Porton gave the following results:

Locality	Speed* mph	Cut-off per cent	IHP
Esher	60	22½	1165
Walton	59	22½	1241
Byfleet	59	22½	1137
Woking	55	25	1199
Farnborough	57	25	1233
Fleet	60	25	1118
Hook	55	25	1186
Basingstoke	55	22½	1160
Oakley	51	22½	1047
Hurstbourne	70	20	1216
Andover	76	20	1223
Grateley	48	25	1048
Porton	70	20	1046

*Speed at which indicator cards were taken.

The coal per train mile averaged no more
than 41.8lb, in maintaining boiler pressure, as
far as Hurstbourne, between the narrow limits of

193 and 203lb/sq in. There was some slight relaxation towards the end of the run, and at Porton pressure was down to 178 lb/sq in. The coal per indicated horsepower hour worked out at 2.2lb, which was almost equal to the 2.1lb/ihp hour registered in the 1924 trials of the GWR 4-6-0 No 4074 *Caldicot Castle,* which caused such a stir when the figures were published later in that year. From the results obtained with the *Sir Lamorak* it was clear that the Southern had got a locomotive design of high efficiency. The mean indicated horsepower from the 14 sets of cards taken between Esher and Porton was 1155.5, at speeds varying between 48 and 76mph. In relation to the nominal tractive effort of 25,320lb this was a very satisfactory performance having regard to its achievement on cut-offs varying entirely between 20 and 25 per cent. In similar conditions of working the GWR 4-6-0 *Caldicot Castle* had produced between 1300 and 1400ihp, which is roughly comparable on a power/tractive effort basis.

Another test with engine No 451 *Sir Lamorak* gave some spectacular results. With the normal load of the Atlantic Coast Express, 10 coaches with a tare weight of 281 tons, the driver was asked to go harder than usual; and go hard he did, to arrive in Salisbury 16min early, to the consternation of the station staff who were quite unprepared. The outstanding feature of this run was a time of 39min from Clapham Junction to Basingstoke, 43.9 miles, against an average rising gradient of 1 in 1000. This effort, involving an average speed of 67½mph would

represent an output of about 900 *drawbar* horsepower. Although the engine was indicated no figures have subsequently been published. So far as the bare details of the run were concerned, Basingstoke was passed in 45½min from the start at Waterloo; Andover in 61min, and Salisbury reached in 76min.

On general observations, however, it soon became clear that the very high standard set by the test performances of *Sir Lamorak* were not being equalled elsewhere, quite apart from questions of record breaking. It was perhaps understandable that from their mass-introduction the new engines would take some getting used to. By outward appearances the Bournemouth men seemed to be coal dodging; though there is another factor that must be taken into account. The permanent way of the old LSWR was not one of the best in Great Britain, any more than was that of the SECR. After the disastrous accident near Sevenoaks in 1927 a number of riding tests were conducted with the 2-6-4 tank engines of K class both on the LNER main line between St Neots and Huntingdon, and on the former LSWR line between Woking and Walton; and on the latter series a King Arthur was included. The chief inspecting officer of railways, Colonel Sir John Pringle had with him as assessors Mr H. N. Gresley, as he then was, and Sir John Aspinall, and while the tank engines ran well on the Great Northern line, they rolled badly on the South Western. Gresley in particular, was quite scathing about the riding of the King Arthur! It was thought

The 10.45 am Golden Arrow Pullman boat express climbing the bank out of Victoria, hauled by engine No 767 *Sir Valence.*

that the rolling was caused by irregular depression of the road, apparently due to the sleepers not being properly packed, and to defective drainage.

The propensity of a weak or unevenly packed roadbed to set up rolling on a large and heavy engine would amply explain the reluctance of some drivers to run hard, even when their trains were late. I was perplexed at the time when runs with the 6.30pm Waterloo to Bournemouth gave maximum speeds rarely exceeding much over 70 mph on the magnificent racing stretch from Litchfield Tunnel down to Eastleigh. Had I been on the footplate the reason might have been more obvious. The SECR section had its track troubles too, chiefly through the use of sea-beach shingle from Dungeness as ballast. It was of course impossible to get really good packing with smooth round stones as with the broken stone used on the LNWR in pre-grouping days, and later adopted as standard on the Southern, with granite from Meldon quarry, in Devonshire.

The South Eastern problems with the King Arthurs, however, were not confined to the track. The Stewarts Lane men handled them in the way they were accustomed with SECR 4-4-0 engines, with a partly opened regulator and a longer cut-off. They were certainly familiar with engines having long-lap, long-travel valves, in the E1 and D1 superheater rebuilds of the Wainwright 4-4-0s, but these engines had Stephenson link motion set in the Great Western style, with a minimum of lead in full gear. Like the Churchward two-cylinder engines they would run like stags under almost any method of handling, but the King Arthurs with Walschaerts gear did not take kindly to it. Furthermore some of those allocated to Stewarts Lane were inclined to be a little shy for steam — a thing unheard of with the engines on the LSW section. There was one particular black sheep, No 764 *Sir Gawain*, so much so that Maunsell's second assistant, H. Holcroft, was instructed to ride on it and try and find out what was the matter. The tests were made on what was then the hardest train of the day, the 10.45am all-Pullman boat train, shortly afterwards christened The Golden Arrow. But the Stewarts Lane men had a more homely name for it, in proper relation to its colour and its weight — the 'White Elephant'!

For the 78 miles from Victoria to Dover Marine the time allowance was 98min, with a maximum tare load of 425 tons. The investigations began in December 1925, and on the first trip the long adverse start up to Knockholt was a continuous struggle for steam, with water level in the boiler being held only at the expense of pressure. Eventually they scrambled over the summit with no more than 115lb/sq in on the gauge, and the engine working in 50 per cent cut-off with full regulator. With no greater hindrance than a moderate permanent way check the train was 4¾min late on arrival at Dover. Several trips gave similar results and eventually the engine was stopped and a thorough examination made. The result was a classic example of how a small variation in detail construction can affect the performance of a steam locomotive. The fact that the engine in question was one of those built by the North British Locomotive Company made the examination all the more searching and interesting. The only variation that could be discerned was a slightly greater camber on the brick arch, which seemed peculiar to engine No 764. So the brick arch was knocked down, and a new one built exactly to match those put in by Eastleigh on the G14 replacements. It worked like a charm, and 764 took its rightful place in the boat train link.

These investigations by Holcroft had another result. Maunsell and Clayton were concerned at the reports of consistent working by the SECR men with partly opened regulators and long cut-offs. Even when maintaining reasonable steam pressure, No 764 had been worked with regulator half open and 33 per cent cut-off for level running, and this was characteristic of Stewarts Lane practice, even with free steaming engines. The general impression was that the engines on the South Eastern were not giving so good an all-round performance as those on the South Western, and so Maunsell decided to have a set of coal trials, between selected Nine Elms and Stewarts Lane drivers. To make things as equal as possible the chosen engines from both sheds were Scotchmen, No 768 *Sir Balin*, and No 778 *Sir Pelleas*, driven respectively by W. Curry, and H. W. Gray. Both men had a period of road learning beforehand and during the actual trials, made on the Golden Arrow and the Atlantic Coast Express the only visitors on the footplate were Rodgers, the test engineer, on No 778 and Holcroft on No 768. There were no road pilots when the men were working over each other's routes, and the two engineers stayed with the same engine and crew throughout. The drivers were given complete freedom to work their engines as they thought best.

As was expected the Stewarts Lane man on No 768 never linked up below 25 per cent either on his own line, or between Waterloo and Salisbury, and eased the regulator back when lighter steaming was required. By contrast, the Nine Elms driver pulled No 778 back to 18 per cent wherever possible, running mostly with a full open regulator. The result, as shown in the adjoining tables, was an outright win for Nine Elms, though strangely enough the disparity was less on the Salisbury road than on the Dover. One could argue that the differences could be accounted for as much by variations between individual engines as in the methods of driving; but the comparison did not extend to running a further series with the Nine Elms crew on No 768, and the Stewarts Lane men on No 778. Apart from the variations in driving methods, Holcroft noted a point of some significance that could well have contributed to the higher coal consumption of engine No 768. In working the boat trains with the D1 and E1 4-4-0 engines, and with the unrebuilt Wainwright types the SECR men had always endeavoured to run with the Ramsbottom balanced safety valves just sizzling, with a feather of steam showing, but always short of full blowing off. This was also normal practice on the Great Western. But with Ross pop safety valves this cannot be done. It is

all or nothing, and when full blowing off occurs there is not only an appreciable loss of steam, but a drop of about 10 lb/sq in in pressure before the valve closes. On No 768 a very free steaming engine, trying to run too near to maximum pressure resulted in frequent blowing off. The average results from the twelve return trips were as follows:

TYPICAL ENGINE WORKING

WATERLOO-SALISBURY : : : 12-coach trains

ENGINE No 453 King Arthur

DIRECTION SCHEDULE (FOR 83.8 MILES)	DOWN 92 min	UP 93 min
Regulator opening	FULL THROUGHOUT WATERLOO TO GRATELEY Eased afterward	¼ and then FULL to Grateley ½ main valve to Oakley Small valve onwards to London suburbs
Cut-offs per cent	To Vauxhall 30 Clapham 25 Malden 27 Weybridge 23 Brookwood 20 Milepost 31 23 Oakley 20 Tunnel Jc. 18	Start to top of 165 50 down to 35 To Grateley 25 Rest of journey 18

COAL TRIALS: ENGINES 768 and 778

Engine No	Total train mileage	Coal* used in running lb	Coal per train mile lb	Water from tender gall	lb of water per lb of coal
SOUTH EASTERN LINE					
768	156	9237	59.6	6382	6.91
778	156	7588	48.6	5192	6.84
SOUTH WESTERN LINE					
768	167.4	8905	53.2	6224	6.99
778	167.4	8084	48.3	5142	6.36

* Hard Yorkshire coal, calorific value 13600 BthU %lb

The coal figures are the average of the week's work for a single round trip. It is interesting to see that the Nine Elms driver's consumption of coal per train mile was almost exactly the same on both routes, whereas the Stewarts Lane man used *less* on the foreign route. On all occasions the trains were made up to a nominal tare load of 415 tons, and the average speeds required were 54.6mph in each direction between Waterloo and Salisbury, and 47.8mph down and 44.5mph up between Victoria and Dover. That as much or more coal was consumed on the latter duties as on the more sharply timed Atlantic Coast Express is a measure of the difficulties of the principal Continental boat train route.

N15 4-6-0 No 744, afterwards named *Maid of Astolat*.

CHAPTER FOUR

THE TROUBLED YEARS

By the early months of 1926 the technical qualities of the King Arthur class locomotives had been well established, and with the alterations to the Urie N15s complete, the Southern Railway had a stud of 60 powerful and reliable engines. But a number of factors other than basic design, construction and maintenance were to harass the locomotive department for several years, and although the best of the day-to-day running was a very good best, particularly on the West of England main line, there was much variation that continued to perplex outside observers. My personal experiences continued to be confined to the Bournemouth line, and during the winter of 1925-6 my runs with the new Scotchmen were on the whole disappointing. My first trip was with No 784 *Sir Nerovens* on the 6.30pm down on a Friday evening, with a load of 385 tons gross. We began well, and were accelerating rapidly on the level from Wimbledon when we were suddenly pulled up by signals, and held for 2min. This seemed to take all the heart out of the running, and certainly did not justify our passing Woking 8¼min late.

The recovery was terribly slow, for it took us more than 10 miles to reach as much as 56mph and we fell to 48mph on the rise to Milepost 31. We did a little better on to Basingstoke, and the minimum speed of 51½mph up the 1 in 249 past Worting Junction was not at all bad. But then, with the grand racing stretch to Eastleigh ahead of us, we drifted downhill at no more than 66mph, and eventually stopped in Southampton in 95min 55sec — 4min late. Had we averaged no more than 73 or 74mph down that long descent,

The first of the Brighton Arthurs, No 793 *Sir Ontzlake*, at Stewarts Lane.

an easy task for so free-running an engine as a King Arthur we could have won back another 2½min. The same lethargic kind of running continued to Bournemouth. A few weeks later when I was on the same train No 791 *Sir Uwaine* did manage to keep time to Southampton, but it was an uninspired trip, with speeds of 62½mph at Esher, 47½mph at Milepost 31, nothing over 65mph on to Basingstoke. This time, after speed had risen to 74mph at Winchester Junction, steam was shut off, and an immediate reduction made to 64mph at Winchester. Onwards from Southampton the work was rather better, but there was not enough time in hand for a permanent way slack through Christchurch, and we were 3min late into Bournemouth.

A return journey on the 8.43am up 2¼ hour train included the same feature of steam being suddenly shut off on a fast stretch of line, without apparent reason. This time the engine was No 787 *Sir Menadeuke,* with a load of 385 tons. The same bridge repair slack at Christchurch affected the first stage, and we lost 4¼min to Southampton. The restart was terribly slow, and at Eastleigh 5.7 miles out, the speed had not risen above 44mph. There was every reason for hustle too, because there was a check to come at Shawford to 33mph. After that the speed on the 1 to 250 ascent rose slowly to 37mph at Winchester, 39 at Winchester Junction and finally to 44mph from Micheldever to the summit. Some brisk running followed; but then, passing Brookwood at 72½mph there came a sudden shutting off of steam, and speed checked to 55mph. We recovered slowly to 69mph below

Byfleet, but signal checks were experienced from Surbiton inwards and we were eventually 12¾min late into Waterloo.

Having learned in later years what these engines could really do, I could have found these early experiences, when the engines were new and just nicely run in, most perplexing—but for one thing. The Bournemouth men traditionally handled their engines on a light rein, and with the soft blast from the use of short cut-offs the exhaust steam came flopping down, and there must have been many times when the look-out ahead was obscured. Those sudden closings of the regulator could well have been out of sheer necessity to see signals. All the same this would not account for the painfully slow accelerations from checks and poor uphill work. My general impressions of that first winter of the King Arthurs on the Bournemouth route was that the running was little better than that of the Drummond D15 4-4-0s, though generally superior to that of the H15 4-6-0s of the 473 series.

Then in May 1926 came the general strike, followed by the prolongation of the coal strike through the entire summer and autumn. The Southern, like the other British railways imported a good deal of coal from Western Europe, but its quality, for locomotive purposes was far below the standard of the best British grades. The Bournemouth engines were generally supplied with Welsh coal, and the foreign stuff brought steaming troubles. In the autumn of 1926 I had a run on the 6.30pm down, with engine No 785 *Sir Mador de la Porte* on which

The 6.30 pm Bournemouth and Weymouth express in Clapham cutting: engine No 792 *Sir Hervis de Revel.*

During the 1926 coal strike: one of the Urie N15s, with improved draughting and Maunsell chimney, No 737 *King Uther*, fitted for oil firing.

boiler pressure at one stage was down to 100lb/sq in. In the meantime the work of the King Arthurs on the boat trains was giving the locomotive department such concern that a suggestion was made to try one of the H15 4-6-0s in the hope that with smaller coupled wheels better time could be made on the banks. But whatever had been done to modify the front ends of the Urie N15 express engines had not been extended to the H15, and after my experiences with the latter class on the Bournemouth route, I was not surprised to learn that the H15 was a dismal failure on the boat trains.

By far the best work in those early years was done on the West of England service run mainly by the top link men at Nine Elms and Salisbury. It was in the summer service of 1926 that the name Atlantic Coast Express was given to the 11am express from Waterloo, and it was amusing that on the attractive poster advertising the train it was shown hauled by No 764, the black sheep of Stewarts Lane, which so far as I know never worked on the service — at any rate in those early years. At first the loads were not much above 300 tons, and details of four runs between Waterloo and Salisbury are tabulated, two in each direction of running. One thing is important to bear in mind. With the introduction of the King Arthurs the practice of engines working through between Waterloo and Exeter, tried for a time with the Urie N15s, was abandoned. Engines and men worked single-home turns both east and west of Salisbury. At this stage too most of the men had their own engines, though in later years there were some double manned rosters.

On the first run tabulated engine No 776 *Sir*

Galagars was in the charge of a well known driver, Collarbone, of Nine Elms, and with what we would later have regarded as a light load, of 325 tons, he ran very well out to Basingstoke, to pass Worting Junction 3½min early despite a permanent way check that cost about 2½min. This run demonstrated that the new engines could handle trains of 300 tons at sustained speeds of well over 70mph on level track, the maxima being 74 past Surbiton, 73 before the Byfleet check and 72½mph near Fleet. Furthermore, the recovery from the permanent way check after Byfleet was most vigorous, to 55mph at milepost 31. After that things could be taken easily, and the driver let 2min of the time in hand slip away between Basingstoke and Salisbury. The second man, with engine No 774

WATERLOO – SALISBURY			
Engine No		776	774
Engine Name		Sir Galagars	Sir Gaheris
Load, tons E/F		310/325	322/340
Dist	Sch	Actual	Actual
Miles	min	m s	m s
0.0 WATERLOO	0	0 00	0 00
3.9 CLAPHAM JUNC	7	6 55	6 55
7.3 Wimbledon		10 40	10 50
12.0 Surbiton		15 20	15 45
19.1 Weybridge		21 30	22 00
–		p w s	–
21.7 Byfleet		–	24 20
24.4 WOKING	29	27 55	26 55
31.0 Milepost 31		35 25	33 55
33.2 Farnborough		37 40	36 15
36.5 Fleet		40 35	39 25
42.3 Hook		45 40	44 55
47.8 BASINGSTOKE	54	50 35	50 15
50.3 Worting Junc	57	53 30	53 15
55.6 Overton		60 05	59 00
66.4 ANDOVER	72	70 05	67 55
72.8 Grateley		76 30	73 20
78.3 Porton		82 35	78 55
–		–	sigs
82.7 Tunnel Junc	87½	86 30	–
83.8 SALISBURY	90	88 35	87 25
Net time min		86	85

The Golden Arrow Pullman boat express hauled by No 769 *Sir Balan.*

Sir Gaheris, showed a steady gain of time throughout, with a clear road, until the train passed Andover 4min early. By the time it was passed even time had almost been attained, but in approaching Salisbury so much ahead of time a check was perhaps inevitable. The individual speeds were not anywhere so high as on the first run until after Basingstoke, when a maximum of 80mph was attained at Andover, and the steep subsequent rise to Grateley was taken at the high minimum speed of 56mph.

The two eastbound runs included some excellent performances. The start out of Salisbury includes the heavy ascent of Porton bank, with four miles at 1 in 169-140, after which comes a switchback section till the fine, even grading of the original London & Southampton Railway is reached at Worting Junction. On the first of the two runs a late start from Salisbury gave Driver Collarbone an opportunity to make some good speed, and by Woking he had regained 5½min of lost time. Speed was 44mph up the 1 in 140 of Porton bank, 82 at Andover, and nothing below 62½mph on the subsequent uphill stretches. The end of the run was spoiled by checks, though with a clear road some 9min of lost time might have been regained. The second run, with No 775 *Sir Agravaine* had a clear road to the very outskirts of Waterloo, and registered an actual gain of 6¼min. As will be told later in

this book, however, times as good as these, and better, were being made by the same engines in the late 1930s with loads of 450 tons!

SALISBURY – WATERLOO					
Engine No			776		775
Engine Name			Sir Galagars		Sir Agravaine
Load tons E/F			285/300		313/330
Dist		Sch	Actual		Actual
Miles		min	m	s	m	s
0.0 SALISBURY		0	0	00	0	00
1.1 Tunnel Junc			3	30	3	40
5.5 Porton			9	45	9	30
11.0 Grateley			16	20	16	35
17.4 ANDOVER		22	21	30	21	45
28.2 Overton			31	00	31	40
33.5 Worting Junc		39	35	30	36	45
36.0 BASINGSTOKE		41½	37	20	38	45
41.5 Hook			41	50	43	20
47.3 Fleet			46	45	48	10
50.6 Farnborough			49	30	51	05
55.8 Brookwood			53	55	55	45
59.4 WOKING		62½	57	00	58	40
–			p w s		–
64.7 Weybridge			62	40	62	50
71.8 Surbiton			69	55	69	10
–			sigs		–
79.9 CLAPHAM JUNC		84	80	25	77	10
–			sigs		sigs
83.8 WATERLOO		92	89	50	85	40
Net times min			83½		85

The final batch of 14 engines of the King Arthur class was turned out from Eastleigh Works between March 1926 and January 1927, and were allocated to the Brighton section. There had been a general increase in train loadings on the principal trains, due to the introduction of new corridor stock and more lavish Pullman facilities; and until the arrival of the King Arthurs the section had only the ex-LBSC types—seven Baltic tanks, the two 4-6-2 tanks, and the eleven Marsh Atlantics. The new batch of King Arthurs had six-wheeled tenders, because the standard bogie type would have made the engine and tender too long for the Brighton section turntables. From all accounts the Arthurs did not go down too well on the Brighton line at first. There was a certain amount of sales resistance to anything that came from the South-Western, and the men found they could not thrash them away from a dead start so readily as they could their own 4-6-4 tank engines. Furthermore, they had the same disadvantage of steam beating down when running linked up, or otherwise steaming easily. The first recorded performances showed no improvement upon the best work of the Baltic tanks.

With the happy relationship that existed between the chief mechanical engineer and the running department, the drifting smoke nuisance was tackled vigorously and comprehensively. It was the first time this trouble had affected British locomotives. Certainly the King Arthurs were not the first to have long lap, long travel valves, and to be driven habitually on short cut-offs; but the high pitch of the boiler, and the relatively short chimney produced a clinging effect from the exhaust which was absent on the

Great Western four-cylinder 4-6-0s, which had a comparable setting of the Walschaerts valve gear. The Churchward two cylinder engines, with the Stephenson link motion were generally driven differently. At the time the Southern was experiencing the smoke nuisance in full measure the Royal Scots had not arrived on the LMS, and the majority of the Gresley Pacifics on the LNER still had their original valve setting.

The first step towards combating the nuisance was taken as early as 1926, when engine No 772 Sir Percivale was fitted with the large German-style side shields, extending upwards to a height of about one foot above the centre line of the boiler. While this was effective, there was some reaction to it on aesthetic grounds. It certainly spoiled the fine front-end appearance of the engine, and during the year 1927 a number of experiments were made with various devices, some weird, and not very effective either. For a time No 772 Sir Percivale, normally a Stewarts Lane boat train engine, was run on the Bournemouth line, presumably for convenience of observation and possible adjustments at Eastleigh. One of the regular Bournemouth engines No 783 Sir Gillemere, was fitted with a strange shovel-shaped device round the chimney. The Bournemouth men had a regular turn to Oxford, via Reading west curve, and I saw No 783 several times on that job. She looked horrible! Another experiment was made on one

Brighton 60-minute non-stop express leaving Victoria: engine No 796 *Sir Dodinas le Savage.*

First steps in smoke-deflecting: No 772 *Sir Percivale* fitted with large German-type shields in 1926.

of the Salisbury engines No 450 *Sir Kay,* with a pair of wings, like those on the winged cap of Mercury, on the chimney.

None of these gadgets however was as effective as the side shields on No 772, and a systematic attempt began to determine to what extent they could be reduced in size, and improved in appearance. At one time in 1927, No 453

King Arthur himself, had small sheets extending only from the raised portion of the running plate above the cylinders to the level of the centre line of the boiler, but the ultimate answer came in a compromise between the arrangements on Nos 772 and 453, with the width of the former and the height of the latter, and a generous rounding of the top, front

Engine No 783 *Sir Gillemere,* with shovel type surround to chimney, at Oxford in 1927.

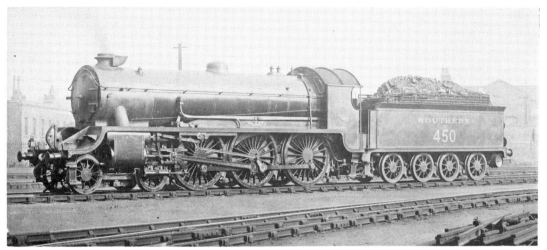

One of the G14 replacements, No 450 *Sir Kay* fitted with wings behind the chimney to assist in smoke deflection.

corner. By the year 1929 the majority of the engines, and also the Urie N15s had this new arrangement, but there was evidently still some inclination to dispense with the side shields if at all possible. In 1930 No 773 *Sir Lavaine* was fitted with a circular projection around the top of the smokebox, and no side shields. By and large, however, the Southern had solved the smoke trouble so far as the King Arthurs were concerned by the time the LMS had the terrible accident to the Royal Scot at Leighton Buzzard in 1931, of which a contributory cause was thought to be the obscuring of the driver's look out due to steam beating down.

At this time a good deal of interest was created on the West of England main line by the running of the first four-cylinder 4-6-0 of the Lord Nelson class. On the basis of tractive effort this engine was vastly more powerful than a King Arthur, and with a nominal figure, at 85 per cent of 33,500lb it was for a few months the most powerful passenger engine in Great Britain. The Nelson was designed to maintain start-to-stop average speeds of 55mph with 500-ton trains; but after the trials on the prototype were complete the authorisation for further construction was limited to 15 locomotives, and with their numbers divided between the Western and

Sir Percivale still had the large deflector shields in 1932 when photographed at Bromley on an afternoon Continental boat express.

the Eastern sections, there were not enough of them to make up all-Nelson links. Consequently the principal express trains had to be loaded to come within the capacity of a King Arthur, that is not exceeding 425 tons tare. The Arthurs thus were never superseded as first line express locomotives. While the Nelsons on their day could do superior work, the Arthurs at their best were so brilliant as to virtually eliminate the difference in tractive effort. It was not until the Nelsons were considerably modified by Bulleid that they strode ahead and took their rightful place in the Southern locomotive stud. But that is another story.

Until the end of Maunsell's tenure of office, the Urie Arthurs, the Maunsell Arthurs and the Lord Nelsons were used turn and turn about. At first the Nelsons were tried west of Salisbury, but this did not continue, and until the advent of the Merchant Navy class, the N15s, Urie and Maunsell alike had the exciting Salisbury-Exeter road to themselves. Although the Urie engines did not have their valve gear altered they were fast, powerful and reliable units though never seeming quite so strong as the true King Arthurs on the banks. One of the Urie engines, No 747 *Elaine,* had the distinction of being the first Southern locomotive to have a maximum of 90mph to her credit. It is not strictly correct to say that this was the first 90 on any part of the Southern system, because as long previously as July 1903 a Billinton Class B4 4-4-0 had reached 90mph near Haywards Heath on a special run from Victoria to Brighton; *Elaine's* 90 was the first in ordinary passenger train service.

Apart from the 90 it was an excellent run throughout, on the up Atlantic Coast Express, and details are given in the adjoining table. To appreciate the excellence of the work reference must be made to the severe gradients of this route, which are more testing to locomotives of eastbound than of westbound trains. The immediate start is up 1 in 100 to Exmouth Junction, and after mounting this vigorously *Elaine* was taken at full tilt down the two mile descent to Broad Clyst to reach 71½mph. Then came the long climb up to Honiton Tunnel, beginning with five miles at 1 in 170-135-100 to Milepost 161¼; a brief respite with a mere mile down at 1 in 100 after Sidmouth Junction, and then the real tug-of-war, beginning at 1 in 100, and steepening to 1 in 90 over the last mile. Yet as will be seen from the table this splendid engine did not fall below 41½mph at Milepost 161¼, touched 64½mph after Sidmouth

EXETER - SALISBURY		
Atlantic Coast Express		
Load: 11 coaches, 330 tons tare, 350 tons full		
Engine: 4-6-0 No 747 Elaine		

Dist Miles	Actual m s	Speeds m p h
0.0 EXETER (QUEEN ST)	0 00	-
1.1 Exmouth Junc	3 25	-
2.9 Pinhoe	5 50	-
4.8 Broad Clyst	7 30	71½
8.5 Whimple	11 05	52
10.3 Milepost 161¼	13 30	41½
12.2 SIDMOUTH JUNC	15 50	-
13.5 Milepost 158	17 15	64½
16.8 Honiton	21 25	34
18.0 Milepost 153½	23 35	31
23.7 SEATON JUNC	29 10	90
27.0 Axminster	31 30	76½
32.1 Chard Junc	36 20	56½
38.5 Milepost 133	44 15	43
40.1 Crewkerne	45 55	80½
45.3 Milepost 126¼	50 15	61
48.9 YEOVIL JUNC	53 25	77½/67
53.5 Sherborne	57 25	71½
56.3 Milepost 115½	61 10	31½
-	sigs	-
59.6 TEMPLECOMBE	65 45	-
-	70 10	-
61.0 Milepost 110½	-	60
64.0 " 107½	76 20	42½
66.4 Gillingham	78 45	68
70.5 Semley	83 45	36½
74.5 Tisbury	88 55	67
78.8 Dinton	92 45	71½
85.5 Wilton	97 55	-
88.0 SALISBURY	101 35	-

Net time   93 minutes

Junction, and entered the tunnel at 31mph. Then, to crown this fine hill climbing, there came the supreme thrill of a full 90mph down Seaton bank. All was then in tremendous form for the long ascent of 13 miles to Hewish summit (Milepost 133). It was not until the train was well above Chard Junction that speed fell below 50mph and then the last two miles, at 1 in 120-160, were carried at a minimum speed of 43mph.

The ultimate standard form of deflector on No 768 *Sir Balin*, passing Ashford on a down boat train in 1928.

Close-up of *Sir Gillemere*, with shovel device, on down Bournemouth express near Hook.

Very fast running was immediately resumed, with maxima of 80½mph below Crewkerne, and 77½mph at Yeovil Junction, and the very stiff Sherborne bank, including a mile of 1 in 80, taken at a minimum speed of 31mph. Then unfortunately came a shocking piece of traffic regulation, for the train was stopped by signals at Templecombe, and kept waiting 4½min for line clear. But this driver was quite beyond discouragement, and on getting the road ran the remaining 28.4 miles to Salisbury in 31min 25sec start-to-stop. His two successive averages were 54.5 and 54.3mph — remarkably fine work with a 350 ton train over a route of such grading severity. Cecil J. Allen estimated that the net time for a normal non-stop run from Exeter to Salisbury was 93min, an average of 56.7mph. I have logged many fine runs of my own over this route, with King Arthurs, but none to equal this in the eastbound direction of running.

During the summer of 1928 the traffic department of the Southern Railway persuaded the locomotive authorities to run some of the West of England expresses with loads of 14 coaches, which, with the new rolling stock then in use, meant tare loads of around 450 tons, and this was a proposition a little too severe even for the King Arthurs on the schedules normally in force. But the Southern had a way of easing out timings at peak holiday periods, so that the trains were apparently late by the public times,

but punctual by the special working arrangements. I had some experience of this on journeys over Bank Holiday periods, both on the West of England and Bournemouth routes. It was nevertheless interesting to see how the locomotives shaped in such conditions of loading, and details are tabulated on a run from Salisbury to Exeter with one of the Urie Arthurs, and a gross load of 480 tons.

SALISBURY - EXETER
Load: 14 coaches, 453 tons tare, 480 tons full
Engine: 4-6-0 No 755 The Red Knight

Dist		Sch*	Actual		Speeds
Miles		min	m	s	m p h
0.0	SALISBURY	0	0	00	-
2.5	Wilton		7	40	-
8.2	Dinton		15	35	52
12.5	Tisbury		21	05	-
17.5	Semley		27	35	38
21.6	Gillingham		31	35	76
-			p w s		
28.4	TEMPLECOMBE	33	39	05	58½
30.8	Milborne Port		43	05	30 (min)
34.5	Sherborne		46	45	77½
39.1	YEOVIL JUNC	44	50	45	-
41.3	Sutton Bingham		53	00	46½ (min)
47.9	Crewkerne		59	50	-
49.8	Milepost 133¼		63	00	28½
55.9	Chard Junc		69	30	-
61.0	Axminster		73	55	74
64.3	SEATON JUNC		77	05	-
69.0	Milepost 152½		88	30	-
70.0	" 153½		91	20	18½
75.8	SIDMOUTH JUNC	84	96	50	76
83.2	Broad Clyst		102	45	82
86.9	Exmouth Junc		106	00	-
-			sig,stop		1½ min
88.0	EXETER (QUEEN ST)	97	110	35	-

Net time   105½ minutes
* Normal schedule

CHAPTER FIVE

THE GREAT YEARS

The over-riding traction policy of the Southern Railway with the impending development of main line electrification resulted in a cut-back on the programme of steam locomotive building in the late 1920s. But it had what could have been more serious repercussions, in that no further funds were made available for the modernisation of steam locomotive servicing and maintenance facilities. The staff had to carry on in dirty, outdated sheds, with superannuated machinery; yet all the time the traffic department was planning accelerated timings. It is true that there was nothing so sensational as the new contemporary services on the other three group railways of Great Britain, but the minutes were being clipped off here and there, and all the time loads were on the increase. It was significant that in the 10 years between 1930 and the outbreak of the second world war the only new express passenger locomotives added to stock were the 40 Schools, while the LMS was engaged in a tremendous programme of 'scrap and build' and a steady build-up of new power was constantly in progress on the Great Western and the LNER.

In the height of the summer season every engine that could turn a wheel was pressed into passenger traffic at weekends. I myself had an unexpected, and remarkably good run with one of the old Drummond T14 four-cylinder 4-6-0s on a relief Bournemouth express. One could not use their old nickname then, because in the second rebuilding, when they received Maunsell superheaters and improved lubrication they also lost their great paddlebox splashers. The attention given to those engines was typical of the circumstances in which the steam locomotive stud had to be operated. It was a case of making do, and it is a great pleasure to be able to recall how the situation seemed to act as a challenge to everyone concerned. At a time when increasingly intense utilisation was taking some of the old-

One of the Maunsell S15 4-6-0s No 834, without smoke-deflectors, and with high sided Lord Nelson style tender.

One of the H15s of 1924-5, No 521, with Maunsell type chimney, but retaining Eastleigh superheater.

time glitter off the stars of the LMS and the LNER, the express locomotives of the Southern were among the smartest looking in the whole country. It was not only Nelsons, Arthurs and Schools that were positively burnished. Relatively minor sheds like Gillingham (Kent) and Tonbridge put a superb finish on to their Wainwright 4-4-0s, and this attitude was reflected in the enterprise of the footplate men.

Mention that every engine that could turn a wheel was pressed in passenger service at summer weekends leads me to a small, but important addition to the King Arthur family that has so far escaped attention. This was the Maunsell development of the Urie S15 class, with 5ft 7in coupled wheels. The new engines, of which 15 were built in 1927, were in every way a mixed traffic version of the King Arthur with the same boiler and firebox, and cylinders and valve motion interchangeable. Because of the smaller coupled wheels they had a considerably higher nominal tractive effort, 29,860lb against

The standard form of the Maunsell S15 with smoke-deflecting plates, and Urie type tender.

25,320lb. Although used on excursion trains, and Saturday reliefs to the regular expresses they were primarily fast freight engines, and worked the heavy night express goods trains between Nine Elms and Exeter, Nine Elms and Southampton and the corresponding up trains. It so happened that my very first footplate trip on a Southern locomotive was on one of these engines, working the up evening fitted goods from Exeter. One can never arrange railway circumstances to the best advantage for loco-motive observation, and it was unfortunate that we had a light load as far as Templecombe — no more than 200 tons — but it gave me an oppor-tunity of appreciating the working of the engine, and her remarkably smooth running on a short cut-off, and narrow regulator opening. But everything changed at Templecombe where the load was made up to 44 vans, vacuum fitted throughout.

The actual gross trailing load was about 500 tons, but in comparing the performance with that of passenger vehicles the considerably higher tractive resistance, in pounds per ton, of four-wheeled freight stock must be taken into account. Our train had 90 axles, whereas a passenger train of equivalent dead weight would

9.44 p m GOODS : : TEMPLECOMBE-SALISBURY
Load: 90 axles, 500 tons full
Engine: Class S15 No 826

Dist Miles		Actual m s	Speeds m p h
0.0	TEMPLECOMBE	0 00	-
2.0	Milepost 110	3 35	48
4.5	" 107½	7 38	31
6.8	Gillingham	10 55	52½
8.9	Milepost 103¼	14 16	29
10.9	Semley	18 55	24½
15.9	Tisbury	26 00	-
20.2	Dinton	31 55	49 (max)
25.9	Wilton	40 30	-
28.4	SALISBURY	47 05	

have only 60. While the loading per axle was lighter, notice must also be taken of the way four-wheeled stock noses about, instead of running smoothly in line. From a number of observations I would have judged that this particular train was pulling around 600 tons of passenger stock. The log of our run to Salisbury is shown in the adjoining table. With three-fifths regulator and 35 per cent cut-off No 826 got away smartly on the 1 in 80 descent. We were doing 48mph at the foot of the bank, fell to 31 on the stiff pull up to Buckhorn Weston

S15 class 4-6-0 No 826 on 7.45 pm up express goods before leaving Exeter on the occasion of the Author's trip.

Engine No 772 *Sir Percivale,* with standard smoke deflecting plates on down Bournemouth and Weymouth express in Winchfield cutting.

tunnel, but on descending to Gillingham the regulator was brought back considerably; even so we accelerated rapidly to 52½mph before striking the four mile climb at 1 in 130-114-100 to Semley. The driver opened out to three-fifths regulator the moment we were through Gillingham; the engine responded well, but half-way up he gave her a bit more still. So, rousing the echoes, we sustained 24½mph up the last mile to the summit—a fine speed this, at a place where the best expresses often dropped below 35mph even though they had the advantage of at least 10mph higher speed through Gillingham. Once

over the top cut-off was reduced to 20 per cent again, and we ran quietly down to Salisbury; in spite of a very small regulator opening, and several spells of coasting, speed hovered around about the 50 mark for many miles, though we did not actually exceed 49mph. The driver judged things very neatly, and brought us into Salisbury passenger station on the stroke of time. From Salisbury our engine was a King Arthur, in somewhat rundown condition. She steamed freely enough, and did the job, but with many checks the performance was not representative of the best that the class could do.

One of the Maunsell S15 4-6-0s, No 833 with six-wheeled tender.

Birkenhead-Bournemouth express (GWR stock) near Southcote Junction: engine No 785 *Sir Mador de la Porte.*

One of the Urie H15s of 1913 No 484 at Waterloo in 1936, with original type of boiler but fitted with Maunsell superheater.

Continental boat express rounding curve on the main line at Orpington Junction: engine No 769 *Sir Balan.*

Maunsell S15 No 834 with standard tender and smoke-deflecting plates on stopping train for Salisbury at Worting Junction.

Engine No 803 *Sir Harry le Fise Lake* leaving Brighton, on 60-minute non-stop express to Victoria.

In studying a great mass of performance data with King Arthurs collected in the 1930s there is little doubt that by far the most enterprising work was done on the Western Section. On the Kent Coast trains their work came to be overshadowed by that of the Schools, and there would be no point in a chronicle of this kind in setting out logs of runs just for the record as it were. When it comes to the Western Section, however, one of the most gratifying features was the great improvement in running, and the much more enterprising attitude on the Bournemouth line. Non-stop running from Waterloo to the best pre-war time of two hours was restored in 1930, and the loads were at first usually kept to ten coaches, making a gross trailing load of about 340 tons. The limit down laid down for these trains was actually 365 tons.

All my runs with the 8.40am up, exclusively on Monday mornings gave indications that the

Continental boat express in Folkestone Warren, hauled by No 771 *Sir Sagramore*—a Scotchman but then fitted with a six-wheeled tender.

A well-known Brighton Arthur, No 799 *Sir Ironside,* at Victoria.

drivers were nursing their engines in the early stages, and to some extent also on the long climb from Eastleigh to Litchfield Tunnel; after which there would come a great sprint for home, making full use of the ability of the King Arthurs to run very fast in light steaming conditions. The Bournemouth non-stops, of 108 miles, were the longest made by the King Arthurs without the chance of taking water, and with a full 5000 gallons in the tender from Bournemouth it would allow about 42 or 43 gallons per mile, leaving something in the tank to get down to Nine Elms shed after arrival at Waterloo. Normal coal consumption on heavy duty was around 45lb per mile, and with an evaporation of about 7lb of water per pound of coal this would correspond to about 35 gallons per mile. In normal circumstances the 5000 gallon tender should have provided an ample margin. On the 6.30 pm down I had runs on which 13 coach trains, with a gross load of 460 tons, were taken down to Southampton on the accelerated time of

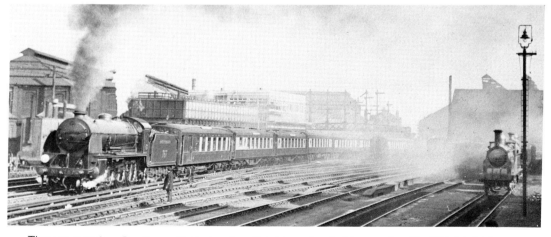

The up evening Southern Belle leaving Brighton, hauled by engine No 767 *Sir Valence,* then with six-wheeled tender. The engine on the extreme right of the picture is a Gladstone 0-4-2 No 172.

87min, for the 79.2 miles, though my best runs on the Bournemouth service were still made on trains worked by Nine Elms men. This was no disparagement to the Bournemouth drivers and firemen; it was simply that the whole standard of running on the Western Section of the Southern Railway had advanced.

On the up road from Salisbury to Waterloo I have tabulated four runs of great interest. The first was on the Atlantic Coast Express with a mid-week load outside the holiday season. With a late start, and an absolutely clear road engine No 777 *Sir Lamiel* was driven to make the extraordinary time of 72min 41sec start-to-stop from Salisbury to Waterloo. This run was indeed so extraordinary as to take some believing. When writing one of my earlier books, I discussed its details with the late Mr H. Holcroft. He was frankly incredulous. In working out some of the details it showed that the engine was working well beyond normal maximum capacity. Now all of us who have made a practice of recording locomotive running know that a skilful driver and fireman can get a substantial extra out of a steam locomotive, temporarily; but on this occasion the crew of No 777 were getting that extra for about an hour on end. This, as Mr Holcroft emphasised to me was so unlikely as to be virtually impossible; and anyone who has read Holcroft's own books will appreciate that no one had a greater knowledge of the technical

working of the King Arthurs than he.

What then is the explanation? An analysis of the running over the 26.3 miles between Winchfield and Esher, with its average speed of 85.8mph suggests an indicated horsepower in excess of 1500. In more recent years tests by British Railways have established some interesting figures for the effects of adverse and favourable winds, and a strong south-westerly wind could quite easily give the driver of an up West of England express a bonus of 150 to 200 horsepower at 80 to 85mph. This would bring the performance of engine No 777 from the highly improbable down to the just possible category. I am not questioning for one moment the veracity of the actual times and speeds made. They were recorded by an observer of long experience and unimpeachable accuracy. It is just that without some further qualification they are inexplicable.

The second run in the table was one of my own recording, with one of the crack Salisbury crews. It began well, and from Grateley summit there was a tremendous acceleration to reach 85mph at Andover. Impetus from this was exhausted on the sharp rise to Milepost $62\frac{1}{2}$, and from there to Oakley the indicated horsepower was well in excess of 1200—top class King Arthur standard. But it was a very hot and sultry day, and beyond Basingstoke we ran into a tremendous storm of thunder, rain, and hail, and the driver eased

Birkenhead-Bournemouth express, between Reading West station and Southcote Junction, engine No 788 *Sir Urre of the Mount.*

SALISBURY-WATERLOO

Engine No:		777		456		776		751	
Engine Name:		Sir Lamiel		Sir Galahad		Sir Galagars		Etarre	
Load tons tare		328		419		419		447	
Load tons full		345		450		445		490	

Dist	Actual	Speed	Actual	Speed	Actual	Speed	Actual	Speed
Miles	m s	m p h	m s	m p h	m s	m p h	m s	m p h
0.0 SALISBURY	0 00	-	0 00	-	0 00	-	0 00	-
1.1 Tunnel Jc	3 04	-	3 48	-	3 49	-	4 24	-
5.5 Porton	8 22	53	10 37	36	9 50	39	11 59	29
11.0 Grateley	14 00	66	18 13	53½	17 00	53½	21 00	46
17.4 ANDOVER Jc	18 43	88½	23 16	85	22 16	78½	26 38	75
21.2 Milepost 62½	-	70½	26 21	61½	25 34	62	30 10	53
22.7 Hurstbourne	22 52	76½	27 42	68½	26 51	68½	31 43	60
24.6 Whitchurch	24 24	72½	29 28	62	28 35	64	33 48	54
28.2 Overton	27 20	72½	32 57	63½	31 53	65	37 53	53
31.4 Oakley	29 54	79	36 04	62	34 50	69	41 29	59
33.5 Worting Jc	31 33	75	38 02	69	36 39	71	43 39	64
36.0 BASINGSTOKE	33 26	88½	40 05	75	38 36	82½	45 52	76½
-	-		storm		-		-	
41.6 Hook	37 25	80	44 53	63	42 46	78	50 26	65
44.1 Winchfield	39 15	82	47 14	63	44 38	76	52 34	69
47.3 Fleet	41 33	85	50 08	-	47 12	79	55 15	75
50.6 Farnborough	44 00	80½	53 05	69	49 50	75	58 06	68
52.8 Milepost 31	-	76½	55 01	68	51 39	72	60 06	65
55.8 Brookwood	47 56	83½	57 36	76½	53 59	80	62 43	72½
-	-		sigs		-		-	
59.4 WOKING	50 26	88½	61 25	30	56 41	80½	65 41	75
62.1 Byfleet	52 15	90	64 35	60	58 41	82	67 51	75
64.7 Weybridge	54 05	82	67 18	53	60 41	69	70 00	68½
69.4 Esher	-		72 02	62½	-	71	74 05	72
71.8 Surbiton	59 28	76½	74 27	56	66 47	67	76 14	63
76.5 Wimbledon	63 20	69	79 32	58½	71 21	58	80 45	64
79.9 CLAPHAM JC	66 27	-	83 17	-	75 07	-	84 27	-
-	-	-	sigs	-	-	-	sigs.	-
83.8 WATERLOO	72 41		93 12		80 40	-	96 17	-

| Net times (min) | 72¾ | | 87½ | | 80¾ | | 91½ | |

considerably, probably because he was not seeing the signals to the best advantage. We were going well again by Farnborough, with 69mph on level track with a 450-ton load indicating around 1250ihp, but further checks hampered the conclusion of the run.

The third run was one of the finest King Arthur performances I have ever seen. Nevertheless while an actual time of 80¾ min, start-to-stop, for a run of 83.8 miles is outstanding on any basis of reckoning for a locomotive of 25,000lb tractive effort with a 450-ton load it must not be forgotten that in the eastbound direction the gradients favour the locomotive. The adjoining table gives the altitudes of various parts of the line above rail level at Waterloo, and the most spectacular stretch, from Grateley to Clapham has an average falling gradient of 1 in 940. In the working of a 450-ton train the gradients provide a gift of 240 horsepower to a King Arthur class engine making, as No 776 did,

an average of 71½mph, while to average 60mph in the reverse direction, 210 horsepower is being exerted in overcoming gravity. In Holcroft's unrivalled experience of the practical working of the King Arthurs he found that the engine resistance could be taken as twice the coach resistance, and on this basis the horsepowers for the two examples quoted work out as overleaf.

Altitudes (ft) above rail level at Waterloo	
Clapham Junction	2.5
Basingstoke	262.5
Oakley	345.0
Andover Junction	215.5
Grateley	371.0
Salisbury	154.5
Average gradient: Grateley-Clapham Junction is 1 in 940	

Both these performances show an average level of indicated horsepower in the 1100 area, corresponding to the heavy workings trials of

King Arthur with 450-ton train:
Clapham Junction-Grateley

Horsepower overcoming

Direc-tion	Average speed mph	Train resist-ance	Engine resist-ance	Gravity	Equiv. draw-bar hp	Indi-cated hp
Down	60	613	354	221+	823	1188
Up	71½	900	525	252−	652	1173

engine No 451 in 1925. The friend who logged the run of No 776 on which the above discussion is based told me that the driver had to push the engine harder than normal to make such fast times; but as normal working on the eastbound run meant cut-offs of less than 20 per cent and the small valve of the regulator, harder than that probably meant he was using the main rather than the small valve. As will be seen from the table there was some magnificently sustained fast running.

The last run in the table was one of my own recording, on a Sunday evening express in mid-summer, when one of the Urie engines had to handle a crowded 14-coach train. As usual with those engines the start was rather laboured, and the time of 21min to Grateley could not be entirely debited to the additional 40 tons of train load. But once past Grateley the running was

quite splendid, and the average speed of 65mph from Grateley to Clapham Junction suggested an average indicated horsepower of about 1000. Over the 48.5 miles from Oakley to Clapham Junction, where the average gradient is 1 in 750 descending the average speed was 67.8mph, with the same output in indicated horsepower. The effort up Porton bank, though not to be compared with the best of the King Arthurs, again showed an output of about 1000 indicated horsepower, and represented a very steady sustained performance throughout. The difference between 1000 and 1150 just about shows the distinction between the Urie N15s and the King Arthurs proper.

In the 1930s the Nelsons were on some of the duties from Nine Elms, and occasionally they would pull off a very brilliant run; but in general they did not rise much above the best levels touched by the King Arthurs, and after some experimental workings they were confined to the section east of Salisbury. During the greatest years of Maunsell locomotive performance the Arthurs, together with the Urie N15s had the Salisbury-Exeter line to themselves. While the non-stop trains, with the rapid fluctuation of speed on the see-saw gradients provided some thrilling experiences for the recorders of train speeds, the services that

Continental express approaching Orpington Junction hauled by No 767 *Sir Valence* with eight-wheeled tender.

Up Atlantic Coast Express passing Seaton Junction: Urie N15 No 740 *Merlin*.

included one or more intermediate stops sometimes involved locomotive work that revealed the capacity of the King Arthurs to climb heavy gradients without the benefit of high initial impetus. One day for example, I joined the 12.24pm departure from Seaton Junction, and logged the run set down in the adjoining table. In climbing to Honiton Tunnel engine No 455 *Sir Lancelot*, accelerated to a sustained 26mph on the 1 in 80 gradient, involving a *drawbar* horsepower of 1170, and then dashed away in characteristic style below Honiton, and again after Sidmouth Junction.

When it came to dashing, however, most of my own records over this route go to that very fast young thing the *Maid of Astolat*. One day she had a 410 ton train on the 4.7pm from Axminster, non-stop to Exeter, and although the minimum speed was 20½mph climbing to Honiton Tunnel, she went like a whirlwind

SEATON JUNCTION-EXETER		12.24 p m	
Load: 12 coaches, 362 tons tare, 385 tons full			
Engine: N15 class 4-6-0 No 455 *Sir Lancelot*			

Dist Miles		Actual m s	Speeds m p h
0.0	SEATON JUNCTION	0 00	-
0.8	Milepost 148½	2 30	21
1.8	" 149½	5 15	22
2.8	" 150½	7 53	23
3.8	" 151½	10 15	26
4.8	" 152½	12 32	26
5.8	" 153½	14 40	29
7.0	Honiton	16 15	58
10.3	Milepost 158	19 05	78½
11.6	SIDMOUTH JUNCTION	20 45	-
3.7	Whimple	5 40	65½
7.4	Broad Clyst	8 35	79
9.3	Pinhoe	10 10	62½
11.1	Exmouth Junction	12 25	-
12.2	EXETER	14 55	-

afterwards touching 88mph at Broad Clyst. On another occasion she took over the 3pm from

KING ARTHUR CLASS — ESTIMATED HORSEPOWER

Engine No	Gross Trailing Load tons	Locality	Speed m p h	Estimated Equiv D H P	Estimated I H P
455	385	Seaton Bank	26	1120	1195
450	450	Grateley	43	1200	1370
773	410	Micheldever	48	990	1235
450	450	Milepost 31	50	1015	1260
456	450	Overton	62	1050	1390
776	445	Winchfield-Esher	75.5	645	1238
751	490	Winchfield-Esher	73.0	665	1222
777	345	Winchfield-Esher	85.8	719*	1519*

* If allowance is made for probable tail wind of 7½ m p h at 45 deg to track I H P = 1330

Waterloo, at Salisbury, making intermediate stops at Templecombe and Sidmouth Junction. With 460 tons she was a bit overloaded on the first section, and lost a little time; but with 350 tons onwards she *flew*, with successive maximum speeds of 83½mph at Sherborne, 79 at Yeovil Junction, 85 at Axminster and 82mph before the Sidmouth Junction stop. How this supremely fast engine performed on a Salisbury-Exeter non-stop is shown in a later table, but her hill-climbing was consistently below the best King Arthur standards.

The one-time boat train engine No 768 *Sir Balin* was transferred to the West of England in 1931 and fitted with an eight-wheeled high-

sided tender of Lord Nelson type, and did much very fine work. I have tabulated a good example on the summer timing of the up Atlantic Coast Express non-stop from Exeter. I have certainly recorded better work from Sidmouth Junction up to Honiton Tunnel, with engine No 449 *Sir Torre* on the winter working of the train; but after Honiton summit the work of *Sir Balin* was superb, with a load of 445 tons. In the reverse direction I have set out details of four non-stop runs. On a fast run over this route one could usually expect to clock six separate maxima of 80mph or more, at Gillingham, before Templecombe, at Sherborne, near Axminster, before Sidmouth Junction, and at Broad Clyst. On runs 2 and 3 the six did not materialise, as No 779 reached only 79mph at Axminster, and No 453 did 79mph at both Gillingham and before Templecombe. Only 79!— but with No 779 on a run including such first-rate hill-climbing that Exmouth Junction (86.9 miles) was passed in 85½min, only a slight signal check at the finish prevented a 60mph start-to-stop run.

As to the individual features of these four splendid runs, the Urie engine, *Maid of Astolat*, was consistently slower on the banks although her downhill speeds were some of the highest, including the 88mph at Broad Clyst. One would have thought that in heavy slogging, as between Seaton Junction and Honiton Tunnel there would have been no difference between the Urie and the Maunsell engines; but the work of No 744 was quite typical, and not a product of one driver's technique. As I mentioned earlier it

EXETER-SALISBURY   12.30 p m   Atlantic Coast Express

Load: 13 coaches, 416 tons tare, 445 tons full

Engine: N15 class, 4-6-0 No 768 Sir Balin

Dist		Sch	Actual	Speeds
Miles		min	m s	m p h
0.0	EXETER	0	0 00	-
1.1	Exmouth Junc	3	4 00	-
4.8	Broad Clyst		8 45	68
12.2	SIDMOUTH JUNC	17	18 12	33½/60
16.8	Honiton		24 35	30½
18.0	Milepost 153½		27 10	25½
23.8	Seaton Junc		33 35	82
27.0	Axminster		36 02	74
32.1	Chard Junc		40 57	56
38.3	Milepost 133½		48 37	42
40.1	Crewkerne		50 40	82
45.3	Milepost 126½		54 57	61½
48.9	YEOVIL JUNC	57	58 10	75
53.5	Sherborne		62 20	62
56.1	Milepost 115½		65 45	32
59.6	TEMPLECOMBE	69	70 35	75
64.1	Milepost 107½		74 37	50
66.4	Gillingham		76 55	65½
70.5	Semley		82 05	35½
79.8	Dinton		91 12	75
85.5	Wilton		96 05	slack
88.0	SALISBURY	98	99 20	-

Down Atlantic Coast Express approaching Honiton Tunnel: engine No 768 *Sir Balin* with Nelson type high-sided tender.

SALISBURY-EXETER

Run No:		1			2			3			4	
Engine No:		744			779			453			768	
Engine Name:		Maid of Astolat			Sir Colgrevance			King Arthur			Sir Balin	
Load tons tare		361			388			420			421	
Load tons full		380			415			450			455	
Dist		Actual	Speed		Actual	Speed		Actual	Speed		Actual	Speed
Miles		m s	m p h		m s	m p h		m s	m p h		m s	m p h
0.0	SALISBURY	0 00	-		0 00	-		0 00	-		0 00	-
2.5	Wilton	6 34	-		5 35	-		6 20	-		6 15	-
8.2	Dinton	13 43	58½		11 40	63		13 15	57		13 05	59
12.5	Tisbury	18 30	54		15 55	-		17 55	-		17 50	53
17.5	Semley	24 21	45½		21 05	52		23 35	45		23 50	42
21.6	Gillingham	27 57	83½		24 25	82		27 10	79		27 30	82
23.9	Milepost 107½	29 46	66		26 18	63		29 05	60		29 19	64
28.4	TEMPLECOMBE	33 23	82		29 55	82		32 45	79		32 55	82
30.8	Milborne Port	36 06	48½		32 30	51		35 25	49		35 30	50
34.5	Sherborne	39 27	82		35 37	85		38 40	82		38 45	85
39.1	YEOVIL JUNC	43 12	75		39 10	-		42 15	-		42 10	77
41.3	Sutton Bingham	45 20	48		41 05	56		44 15	50		44 05	54
47.9	Crewkerne	52 08	68		47 05	71		50 50	66		50 15	71
49.7	Milepost 133¼	54 49	32½		49 15	42		53 23	36		52 45	37
55.9	Chard Junction	60 48	77½		54 50	-		59 17	-		58 25	80
61.0	Axminster	64 42	82		58 40	79		63 08	80		62 00	86½
64.2	Seaton Junc	67 21	65		61 20	-		65 45	-		64 30	71
69.0	Milepost 152½	76 10	19		68 50	25		73 40	23		71 30	26½
70.0	Milepost 153½	78 43	26		71 01	29		75 50	27		73 31	32
71.2	Honiton	80 15	60		72 25	-		77 25	-		74 50	62
75.8	SIDMOUTH JUNC	84 03	83½		76 10	80		81 05	82		78 35	82
-		-	69½		-	68		-	71½		-	65
79.5	Whimple	87 03	82½		79 15	-		84 00	-		81 50	76
83.2	Broad Clyst	89 40	88		82 00	80		86 35	86		84 30	83
86.9	Exmouth Junc	92 45	62½		85 35	-		-	-		-	-
-		-	-		sigs	-		89 25	-		87 45	-
88.0	EXETER	94 51	-		88 10	-		92 00	-		90 00	-

Up West of England express passing Crewkerne, with engine No 448 *Sir Tristram*.

One of the G14 replacements, No 457 *Sir Bedivere,* on the up Atlantic Coast express at Exeter Central.

was not the first occasion on which *Maid of Astolat* had taken me through Broad Clyst at 88mph. The second run, with No 779 *Sir Colgrevance,* was distinguished by a most brilliant start out of Salisbury, and by a big sustained effort that made level time soon after Yeovil. At Hewish Summit, milepost 133¼, No 779 was 3½min ahead of the next fastest engine; this advantage was gained chiefly by such grand uphill efforts as 52mph over Semley, and 42 at Hewish itself. Of course the output of power that produced such an average speed as 58.2mph over the five miles from Tisbury to Semley—five miles including 1¾ at 1 in 270 and 2¼ at 1 in 145—could not have been sustained by an engine of such moderate size as a King Arthur, and the downhill stretch to Templecombe was no doubt used for recovering breath. The rate of acceleration from Semley was much swifter with *Maid of Astolat,* which had been driven more easily uphill from Wilton, and between Gillingham and Templecombe the *Maid* actually gained on *Sir Colgrevance.*

On run No 3 *King Arthur* himself, with a 450-ton train, did splendidly throughout: not so fast as *Sir Colgrevance* in the early stages, but with good hill-climbing and a very fast finish a clear 6min was gained on booked time—giving an average speed of 57.3mph from start to stop. Actually the maximum speed at Broad Clyst did not quite equal that attained by *Maid of Astolat,* but *King Arthur* came over the hump between Sidmouth Junction and Whimple at rather higher speed. The average speed between Honiton and Exmouth Junction, 15.7 miles, was 78.6mph against 75.5 by engine No 744. The last of the four runs included some of the finest work of all. No 768 *Sir Balin* dropped slightly behind *King Arthur* in the earlier stages, and at Templecombe he was only half a minute ahead of *Maid of Astolat.* But from that point onwards a really phenomenal effort began. Despite the heavier load of 455 tons, against 415, No 768 kept practically level with No 779 as far as Seaton Junction, and then the engine with the heaviest load made the fastest climb of all up Honiton Bank. From Seaton Junction the gradient is 1 in 80 continuously to the tunnel entrance, marked by milepost 152½ where it eases to 1 in 132 through the tunnel itself. Yet after the hard running that had preceded the climb the engine was driven uphill to such effect as to pass the 152½ milepost at 26½mph and to recover through the tunnel to 32. If one takes the time of *Sir Colgrevance* to Chard Junction, that of *Sir Balin* onwards to Honiton, and that of *King Arthur* to Exmouth Junction the extraordinary aggregate of 83min 15sec from Salisbury is attained. This can be improved by a further four seconds by substituting the times of *Maid of Astolat* from Gillingham to Templecombe. The summary time from Salisbury to Exeter thus becomes 85min 17sec, an average of 61.8mph. One could hardly wish for a finer collective tribute to the capacity of the King Arthur class engines, nor to the enterprise and skill of their drivers and firemen.

CHAPTER SIX

NEW BROOM — THEN WAR

In the summer of 1937 Maunsell retired, and was succeeded by O. V. S. Bulleid, until then Personal Assistant to Sir Nigel Gresley, on the LNER. It was well known that Bulleid, if not the actual architect, was the enthusiastic developer of some of the more spectacular aspects of LNER locomotive practice during the 1930s, though hitherto his exuberance had been held in check by the strong personality of the Chief. All the same, knowing how steam matters on the Southern had been subjugated to electrical developments the connoisseurs wondered what kind of a remit Bulleid would be given. Maunsell's two assistants, Clayton and Holcroft, remained in office, though were given little to do. Clayton's main contribution to the new regime was incidental, and so far as he personally was concerned almost accidental.

During the second world war he wrote an article on the famous Paget sleeve-valve locomotive, with which he had been connected in his pre-SECR days, at Derby. That article, published in *The Railway Gazette* provided the inspiration for Bulleid's notorious *Leader* class tank engines, which eventually exerted the kind of leadership associated with the Duke of Plaza Toro!

Bulleid was not interested in the King Arthurs. One can imagine they were too simple and straightforward for his ingenious and complicated personality, and apart from painting them in his startling malachite green, and changing the style of lettering on their tenders and cab sides they were left alone. His early attentions were justifiably concentrated on the Nelsons, and his remedies for their short-comings were a good deal more drastic than

Bulleid style of painting: No 746 *Pendragon* on up West of England express passing Hersham.

In Malachite Green, No 766 *Sir Geraint* with number only on the cab panels.

outward appearances would suggest. It must however be emphasised that he took office on the Southern when plans for further electrification were in full swing, and although he was soon engaged in plans for a super express passenger steam locomotive design for the Continental trains Sir Herbert Walker was not likely to authorise any large capital investment in steam, any more than he had done for Maunsell. The early days of Bulleid on the Southern were as much a case of making do, and mending, as previously, and with the King Arthurs continuing in their solid, economical and reliable way, they were not engines to need anything except routine maintenance. There would not have been much change when Gilbert Szlumper succeeded Sir Herbert Walker as General Manager; but the war changed everything.

All thoughts of further electrification were put on one side, and once traffic in connection with the despatch of the British Expeditionary Force in the autumn of 1939 was completed, the Southern experienced a considerable recession in passenger business. The Continental workings had ceased. Lord Nelson class engines previously stationed at Stewarts Lane were transferred to Nine Elms, and a further distribution of the King Arthurs took place, little more than two or three years after that which followed the Portsmouth electrification in 1937/8 which had resulted in Schools class 4-4-0s previously at Fratton being transferred to Bournemouth. In the summer of 1939 the latter shed retained only two of the original allocation of Scotchmen, seven of which had gone to Exmouth Junction. The allocation of the whole class then was:

Nine Elms:	736-742
	772-780
Salisbury:	448-457
	747-748
Exmouth Junction:	743-744
	786-792
Eastleigh:	749-755
Bournemouth:	745, 746
	784, 785
Stewarts Lane:	763-769
	781-783
	793, 794
	798, 799
Dover:	770, 771
Ramsgate:	795-797
	800-806

One of the first wartime moves was to allocate some of the Stewarts Lane Scotchmen to Hither Green for heavy goods working, and in exchange for nine Nelsons, previously on boat train workings Nine Elms transferred seven King Arthurs to Stewarts Lane. About the same time also, Bournemouth lost its last two remaining Scotchmen 784 and 785, also to Stewarts Lane. Nine Elms sent two of its Urie N15s, 741 and 742, to Eastleigh. The Stewarts Lane engines were employed on general duties, including interchange workings with other companies.

The most interesting technical development of the early war years was the rebuilding of Urie N15 No 755, *The Red Knight,* with a multiple-jet blastpipe and enlarged chimney. This device had proved successful on the Lord Nelsons, though the rebuilding in the case of No 755 did not also include the provision of entirely new cylinders, as it had done in the Nelsons. A number of the Schools engines had similarly been modified by Bulleid. It may, or may not have been significant that the first application of this form of blastpipe on an N15 should have been made on one of the Urie engines, which by consistent reputation were not so effective as the King Arthurs proper, in climbing heavy gradients. A few additional engines of the Urie series were similarly equipped subsequently, including 736, 737, 741, and 752; but the circumstances of wartime were not favourable to obtain comprehensive data as to the effectiveness of the change. It was reported at one time that the first of those converted, No 755, was in the Nelson link from Nine Elms; but the loadings were fixed so that they could be worked by King Arthur class engines in any case, if a Nelson was not available.

Not a great deal of individual notetaking of engine movement was taken during the war. The King Arthurs were much involved in the evacuation from Dunkirk, though anyone noting details on those hectic and momentous days would probably have been pounced upon as a suspicious character and placed behind bars! By the middle of the war, when the virtual cessation

of new engine building elsewhere had caused something of a shortage in motive power, seven Southern 4-6-0s of the King Arthur family were loaned to the Great Western, and stationed at Old Oak Common. There was one H15, No 478, and four of the original Urie S15s, Nos 496 to 499. With them went four of the rebuilt Brighton Baltics, then 4-6-0s and classified N15X. They were put on to certain important through night goods trains. For Great Western operating purposes they were classified as red route engines—that is they could go anywhere that a Castle, a Hall a 28XX 2-8-0 or a 47XX 2-8-0 could go.

By the end of 1942 some of the King Arthurs were getting much farther afield. Expert observers were mystified at first seeing some of them working coal trains in the Doncaster area, while others were noted on Great Central section goods trains on the GW & GC Joint Line out of London. These movements were evidence of the engines working their way to Heaton shed, Newcastle, where 10, on loan to the LNER, were based for some time. All the engines thus

The look of austerity! Engine No 450 *Sir Kay,* in black and not clean, on down Bournemouth express at Battledown Junction.

A Urie N15, No 755 *The Red Knight* with multiple-jet blast pipe, and all-black wartime livery.

transferred were of the Urie series:

739	King Leodegrance
740	Merlin
742	Camelot
744	Maid of Astolat
747	Elaine
748	Vivien
749	Iseult
750	Morgan le Fay
751	Etarre
754	The Green Knight

It will be noted that none of those sent north had multiple jet blastpipes, though several of them have already featured individually in this book of mine. For structural and weight restriction purposes they were passed to work to Edinburgh and Glasgow, but I doubt if the Geordie drivers gave the sprightly *Maid of Astolat* a chance to develop her normal speed — down Cockburnspath bank, for example! So far as I can ascertain they were employed exclusively on freight trains. An enthusiast travelling to Edinburgh on 30 June 1942, saw No 749 at Dunbar, in the old Southern green livery, and 'looking unusually clean for wartime'.

Quite apart from such organised transfers as the above there were some queer temporary movements to be noted, as when an unspecified King Arthur, based at Hitchin, of all places, was seen working an 80-wagon freight train at Tonbridge, and one of the Scotchmen, No 774, was also seen far up the Great Central line. On the Southern itself, the need for civilians to get some sort of holiday, and the almost complete embargo on pleasure-motoring, led, in 1942, to increased summer train services to the West of England, and eight King Arthurs were transferred from Stewarts Lane to Nine Elms for this

traffic. For the record the engines concerned were 766-770, and 783-785. There were also numerous brief movements to meet the fluctuating exigencies of wartime conditions, and the examples quoted are typical rather than constituting a completely comprehensive account of transfers and temporary loans. It is remarkable however that despite the vulnerable position of the Southern Railway towards enemy air attack, not only in the great blitz of 1940-1, but during the flying bomb, and rocket attacks of 1944-5, that not one of the 74 King Arthur class 4-6-0s was damaged. Among express passenger engines on the Southern the only total loss was one of the T14 Paddleboats No 458, which suffered a direct hit, while berthed in Nine Elms shed.

I resumed my own footplate work just before VE day in 1945, and it was in conditions little removed from those of wartime that I made my first runs on King Arthurs in passenger service, except that the hazards of enemy attack were no longer prevalent. On the Bournemouth line the crew workings were considerably changed from those of pre-war days, with Eastleigh shed taking a share, and the new experience, for me, of seeing locomotives remanned in the course of the run from Waterloo to Bournemouth. In 1945-6 I rode locomotives in many parts of Great Britain, and had a great variety of experiences, but with the King Arthurs the thing that remains the most abiding memory is that of their solid dependability and capacity to stand up to any amount of hard service, and lengthy mileages between repairs. I met Bulleid on several occasions and he was always very friendly towards my literary work; but when I sent him the draft of one article that praised the King Arthurs, it was returned to me with the word 'modern' crossed out, because, as he put it, those engines could not in any circumstances be called modern! It is true that then the youngest of them was then nearly 20 years old, but at the same time as I made these runs I was also riding the first of Bulleid's own West Country lightweight Pacifics, which of course were his pride and joy, and *very* modern.

Reference to these latter engines may seem a little out of place in a book dealing specifically with the King Arthur family, but it so happened that for more than 10 years afterwards a state of co-existence between the West Country and the King Arthur classes existed, particularly on the Eastern Section, and the relationship between the two needs some explanation. With the electrification programme halted during the war, and the likelihood of difficult conditions prevailing for some years afterwards, Bulleid obtained authority for an extensive programme of new steam locomotive construction. It was remarkable, however, in that it embodied no policy of scrap and build, as pursued in the Stanier era on the LMS, or an ordered programme of replacement, as followed on the Great Western. On the Southern, in addition to the 30 express passenger Pacifics of the Merchant Navy class authority was given for the construction of no fewer than 110 of the light-weight variety—*one hundred and ten* new Pacifics! It is probably an exaggeration to say that the arrival of the new engines, in such numbers, was an embarrassment to the Running Department, but to outward appearances there was some difficulty in making use of so many, some of which were put on to the lightest of duties.

More particularly to this book, however, there was fortunately no extensive scrapping of King Arthurs, nor, surprisingly enough, of many much older and less powerful express passenger classes, of ex-LSW and ex-SEC designs. My first footplate experiences in the immediate after-math of the war were on the Bournemouth line, and my first trip was on the 6.20pm Sunday train from Waterloo, booked non-stop to Southampton in 100min. With a load of 420 tons behind the tender this might seem easy work compared to pre-war standards, but the operating conditions were very different. While in the great days of the later 1930s it was almost a hanging matter to delay a fast express train, with all the complications of wartime and post-war traffic passenger trains had not yet been accorded their former priorities. The checks that

occurred, which were often frequent and severe, gave enterprising drivers a chance to run harder than the overall schedules might have appeared to demand, and this first trip of mine was a notable example. The engine was No 772 *Sir Percivale*, smartly turned out in the plain black painting style of wartime, and with Eastleigh men in charge. We had not proceeded far out of Waterloo before I could sense that we had a good engine, but we were also immediately involved in signal checks, which continued with varying severity until we were all but stopped approaching Walton; as will be seen from the log we took just 30min to pass that station, 17.2 miles out. Up till then there was little chance to form any general impression of the engine, except that she was strong in the way this 420-ton train was accelerated from successive checks. Furthermore, the demands for steam were so intermittent that no appreciable test of the steaming capacity of the boiler had so far been applied. But from Walton, except for one moderate signal check at Winchfield we got a clear road right through to Eastleigh, and engine and crew did some excellent work, fully up to pre-war standards.

The King Arthurs are that breed of loco-motives that seem to run equally well on a diversity of handling methods, and while theoretically the correct way to drive was with the reverser pulled up to about 18 per cent cut-off and to use a fully opened regulator wherever possible, this driver obtained first class results on a very moderate coal consumption although never working at less than 35 per cent. The engine steamed freely, rode well, and even when going hard uphill, had a remarkably quiet exhaust beat, with not a trace of fire-throwing. From the virtual stop at Walton the driver used 45 per cent cut-off to get under way, gradually reduced to 35 per cent just after Weybridge. By then speed had risen to 53mph and on the long rise to milepost 31 the deceleration was very gradual; on the long 1 in 314 stretch above Woking 50mph was steadily maintained. I estimate that the drawbar horsepower was around 920, and the indicated horsepower of about 1160 was right up to the standard established in the trials on engine No 451, in 1925, when at this particular location the indicated horsepower was 1179, with the engine working in 25 per cent cut-off, with full regulator. On my trip *Sir Percivale* had 35 per cent and three-fifths regulator.

On the level from Sturt Lane Junction speed was worked up to 60mph, exactly as No 451 had

6.20 p m (Sunday) WATERLOO-SOUTHAMPTON
Load: 382 tons tare, 420 tons full (packed)
Engine: 772 Sir Percivale
Driver: Andrews, Fireman: Bartlett (Eastleigh)

Dist Miles		Sch min	Actual m s	Speeds m p h
0.0	WATERLOO	0	0 00	
-			sigs	
3.9	CLAPHAM JUNC	8	8 50	
-			sigs	
7.3	Wimbledon		14 14	
-			sigs	
12.1	Surbiton		22 24	
-			sigs	
17.2	Walton		30 00	5
19.2	Weybridge		33 20	53
24.4	WOKING	34	39 31	52
28.1	Brookwood		43 52	50
31.0	Milepost 31		47 25	48
33.3	Farnborough		50 05	-
36.5	Fleet		53 25	60
-			sigs	
39.8	Winchfield		58 05	40
42.3	Hook		61 22	58½
47.9	BASINGSTOKE	60	67 50	-
50.4	Worting Junc	63	70 50	46½
52.7	Woolton Box		73 58	46
58.2	Micheldever		79 31	65
66.7	WINCHESTER	84	86 30	72½
69.8	Shawford		89 01	76
-			sigs	
73.6	EASTLEIGH	91	93 56	30
78.2	Northam Junc		99 40	-
79.3	SOUTHAMPTON	100	102 25	-

Schedule 100 min   Net time 87½ min

done 20 years earlier, but the check at Winchfield brought us down to 40mph briefly. Recovery was rapid once again, and we touched 58½mph before entering the six mile climb at 1 in 249 that extends almost to Wootton signal box. With cut-off increased to 38 per cent speed did not fall below 46mph. Here my estimates of the horsepowers were, equivalent drawbar, 1000; indicated, a little over 1200 — again fully up to the best standards of 1925. I should mention that we had some good hard Yorkshire coal on the tender, and the steaming continued very freely. Boiler pressure was kept a little below the rated 200lb/sq in to avoid full blowing off. Although we were 7¾min late passing Basingstoke, on clearing Wootton summit in 73½min we had 26min left for the remaining 26.7 miles down to Southampton, and with a clear road could have kept time comfortably despite the badly delayed start out of London, and the subsequent downhill running was very interesting to observe.

Though continuing with 35 per cent cut-off the regulator was eased back considerably, and I noted that despite the light steaming there was no tendency for the exhaust to beat down and obscure the lookout. On the long 1 in 252 descent speed rose steadily, until it reached 76mph at Shawford. All the time the engine was riding very smoothly, and when we passed Winchester with 13½min left to Southampton it seemed probable that we should make a punctual arrival. But the signal check at Eastleigh spoiled our chances, and although on arrival the station clock at Southampton pointed to 8.1pm our actual time from Waterloo was 102½min. The net time however was not more than 87½min, practically up to the fastest start-to-stop allowance in pre-war days. It was an excellent and most enjoyable trip, showing a King Arthur fully in its old form despite the intermission of six years of war.

My second post-war trip was equally interesting in that we had one of the Urie engines back from its sojourn in the North Eastern Area of the LNER, and moreover fitted with a boiler carrying a pressure of 200lb/sq in. Thus except for retaining the original short-lap, short travel valves, No 747 *Elaine,* was in every sense a King Arthur. The train was the heavy 11.30am from Waterloo, making intermediate stops at Basingstoke, Micheldever and Winchester within an overall allowance of 113min to Southampton. We had a packed 16 coach weighing at least 495 tons gross behind the tender. Again we had Eastleigh men, and with coal of poorer quality than that we had on *Sir Percivale* there was need for careful firing, and judicious handling generally, both of which were forthcoming in the highest degree. Again we had a somewhat delayed start out of London, by having to take the local line, and slow to 20mph to cross to the main line at Wimbledon.

11.30 a m WATERLOO- SOUTHAMPTON
Load: 443 tons tare, 495 tons full (packed)
Engine: 747 Elaine
Driver Billett; Fireman Alexander, to Winchester
Driver Biles; Fireman Abraham, to Southampton

Dist Miles		Sch min	Actual m s	Speeds m p h
0.0	WATERLOO	0	0 00	
3.9	CLAPHAM JUNC		8 21	
7.3	Wimbledon		13 15	20*
12.1	Surbiton		19 45	54
14.6	Esher		22 15	66
17.2	Walton		24 43	61½
19.2	Weybridge		26 37	66
24.4	WOKING	32	31 32	60
28.1	Brookwood		35 45	eased
31.0	Milepost 31		39 30	44
33.3	Farnborough		42 21	easy
36.5	Fleet		46 00	-
42.3	Hoc'k		52 42	-
47.9	BASINGSTOKE	62	60 44	-
2.5	Worting Junc		6 06	34
4.8	Wootton Box		9 56	38
8.3	Litchfield Box		14 36	53/60
10.3	Micheldever	16	17 27	-
2.0	Milepost 60¼		3 49	56
3.7	Wallers Ash East		5 31	64
6.4	Winchester Jc		7 50	75
8.5	WINCHESTER	11	10 00	-
3.1	Shawford		5 09	-
6.9	EASTLEIGH		8 34	72
11.5	Northam Junc		13 31	-
12.6	SOUTHAMPTON	18	16 27	-

The 11.30 am Bournemouth and Weymouth express near Battledown Junction, hauled by Urie N15 No 747 *Elaine* with the Author on the footplate.

Once on the main line the engine was linked up to 27 per cent cut-off, and the regulator opened to just a shade short of full, and the controls were not then touched for the next 20 miles. The response was fine, with speed rising to 66mph on the level past Esher; after a slight drop in Oatlands cutting it reached 66mph again after Weybridge. Here was one of the Urie N15s developing around 1200 indicated horse-power, but with the poor coal the fireman was having a busy time of it, and with time lost by the initial delays made up as early as Woking the driver could afford to ease up a little. Nevertheless, boiler pressure did not fall below 160lb/sq in and things were taken relatively easily on to Basingstoke, where we were 1¾min early. I estimate a net time of 58min for this first stage.

On leaving Basingstoke I saw for the first time another characteristic feature of these fine engines. With the reverser in full forward gear the driver opened straight out to absolutely full regulator, and the engine moved away without a trace of slipping. This I found afterwards was not due to any special skill, or finesse on Driver Billett's part. A few years later when I was given the opportunity of driving a King Arthur myself, I tried the same method of starting, actually on No 768, and she walked away for me just as smoothly and surefootedly—and I am no expert

driver! From Basingstoke on No 747, cut-off was quickly shortened to 50 per cent, and then at milepost 48½ to 35 per cent. *Elaine* was certainly talking as she lifted her 495-ton train up the 1 in 249 gradient, and at the top of the bank, when we were still accelerating and doing 38mph the equivalent drawbar horsepower was about 1030, and the indicated around 1200. When one recalls the halting progress of the Urie N15 engines in their original condition, the spectacle of No 747 thundering up that gradient with the pressure gauge needle stock-still at 190lb/sq in was indeed a revelation of the improvements wrought during Maunsell's time.

Neither were these impressions over when we topped the summit at Litchfield Tunnel. The regulator remained fully open until time to shut off for the stop at Micheldever, and the subsequent run to Winchester was made with full regulator throughout, and 27 per cent cut-off from a point about 200yd from the dead start. Full regulator and 27 per cent up to 75mph was tremendous going, and it won us back a minute of the time lost on the very sharp allowance of 16min from Basingstoke to Micheldever. Indicator diagrams if taken at Winchester Junction would probably have shown something in excess of 1500ihp, though the boiler would not have been able to sustain this for long.

CHAPTER SEVEN

BUSY UNDER NATIONALISATION

The King Arthur family of locomotives came under national ownership with their strength intact. Once the new liveries were decided the N15 class units were painted in passenger colours, similar to the old Great Western style, and the H15s and S15s in black. In this the King Arthurs were more fortunate than the Schools, which had to put up with lined black, in the old LNWR style. To their Southern Railway running numbers were added 30,000. In view of the massive influx of new Bulleid Pacifics on to the Southern it might, at this distance in time, be wondered how the 78 King Arthurs were employed; but in this some considerable reference is needed to the passenger traffic situation in the first 10 years after the end of the war. It was something that had not been approached in pre-war years.

For the first time in national history the ordinary payroll man received holidays with pay. Secondly petrol was still rationed, and, moreover, cars were at first beyond the means of those enjoying for the first time holidays with pay. In the long tradition of seaside landladies bookings were made only from Saturday to Saturday, with the result that a positive deluge of passenger traffic fell upon the railways at weekends. It was no use trying to run the ordinary service with duplication of some of the most popular trains; the whole timetable had to be recast.

On the Southern it meant that far more locomotives than those needed for the weekday service had to be kept in running order, and the enginemen's rosters so worked out that every man on the strength was available for daytime duty on those hectic Saturdays. Men from the country sheds travelled up to London on the cushions, to work outward bound expresses. At sheds like Nine Elms and Stewarts Lane this was the reason for having many King Arthurs available to supplement the Bulleid Pacifics. I shall never forget the breakfast time scene at Stewarts Lane on one such day. In the course of

The first British Railways style: No 30448 *Sir Tristram* on up West of England express at Raynes Park.

Up West of England express passing under Battledown Flyover, in 1960: engine No 30451 *Sir Lamorak,* then fitted with Urie tender.

one single hour *eight* West Country Pacifics, and three King Arthurs left the shed, while in the half hour from 9.15am six more King Arthurs were booked to leave. One after another they set off tender first for Victoria, each dead on their booked time – and, I may add, all very smart and clean.

At the same time Waterloo would be sending off a long distance train on an average every five minutes from 7am and until 2pm. The only ones not then requiring a steam locomotive were the Portsmouth electrics, and every Nelson, King Arthur and even H15 that could be found was pressed into service. At Eastleigh shed there was always an element of uncertainty. The time had not yet arrived when the majority of overseas travellers went by air, and special trains for ocean liner passengers would have to be run often to the number of three for a single liner's arrival at Southampton, equally with uncertainty as to what the actual times of departure might be. King Arthurs shared these jobs with a few of the Lord Nelsons. These trains, like the summer holiday Saturday workings from Victoria and Waterloo did not ordinarily demand any very high performance. It was a case of keeping in the timetable paths. For the boat trains from Southampton, like those from Dover and

Folkestone, there were numerous conditional paths in the working timetable, and boat specials were dispatched from the quaysides to take up the first available path. I remember riding the engine of a special from the *Queen Elizabeth,* when we took a path sandwiched between the first and second sections of the Royal Wessex, the regular morning express from Weymouth and Bournemouth to Waterloo.

To minimise shunting and stock movement many of the summer Saturday trains to and from the Kent Coast were scheduled as rounders which ran out from London serving stations on the Chatham line, and having reached Ramsgate, after a short interval to clean the fire and take water, continued via Minster to Deal and Dover to provide an up service to London, via Folkestone. Similar rounders were operated in the reverse direction. On the West of England main line, west of Salisbury, King Arthurs were used on Saturday reliefs almost to the end of the steam era. These were the kind of duties on which King Arthurs were employed in their last years. For the record the engines that I saw booked off Stewarts Lane before 10am on that one particular Saturday morning were:

30764	*Sir Gawain*
30765	*Sir Gareth*

Newcastle-Bournemouth express near Oxford, hauled by engine No 30782 *Sir Brian.*

30766	*Sir Geraint*
30768	*Sir Balin*
30769	*Sir Balan*
30771	*Sir Sagramore*
30773	*Sir Lavaine*
30794	*Sir Ector de Maris*
30795	*Sir Dinadan*

An interesting point to emphasise about the King Arthurs, in the days after nationalisation is that apart from painting they remained unchanged from their original condition. Many famous locomotive classes have had long lives, but have had incidental, if not major changes in detail, in the cause of standardisation, for example modified chimneys and domecovers; Belpaire, instead of round topped fireboxes, and such like. But the King Arthurs remained unscathed, as it were, apart from various incidental, and non-significant changes of tender. Originally there had been three types of tender. There were the inside-framed Drummond water carts inherited from the G14 four-cylinder engines; the Urie eight-wheelers supplied with the 30 Scotchmen, and the six-wheeled high-sided Maunsell type on the 14 engines allocated to the Brighton line. As time went on some were

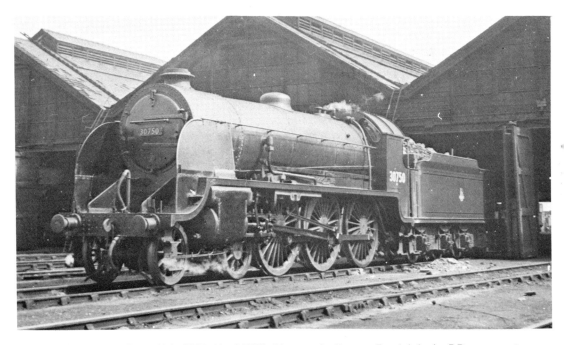

Last years for a Urie N15: No 30750 *Morgan le Fay,* at Eastleigh, in BR green.

At Waterloo in 1957: engine No 30790 *Sir Villiars* on semi-fast train for Southampton.

interchanged particularly as certain Scotchmen were transferred to the Brighton section. Almost at the start of its life engine No 449 *Sir Torre* was fitted with a Urie tender, when it was selected to represent the latest practice of the Southern Railway in the pageant of locomotives at the railway centenary celebrations at Darlington in 1925. For a time No 768 *Sir Balin* had a high-sided bogie tender of the Nelson type, after the engine was transferred from Stewarts Lane to the West of England.

In off-peak periods the King Arthurs at Stewarts Lane shed worked the intermediate Kent Coast passenger trains. Some involved really hard work, not in normal express running but in the sharp intermediate timings between the many station stops. I spent an afternoon and evening on engine No 768 *Sir Balin,* working the 3.35pm London to Ramsgate and returning with the 7.45pm up, due into Victoria at 10.20pm. The only sustained fast running in each direction was between Bromley South and Chatham, and here, with loads of around 300 tons, the schedules were the easiest to observe. The 79.3 miles between Victoria and Ramsgate were scheduled in 2hr 33min out, and 2hr 35min on the return; but the 12 intermediate stops were between them booked 23min standing out and 24min on the return, which latter included an extra stop, at Gillingham, which was not made on the outward run. The running averages of 36.5 and 36.3mph involved infinitely harder work than plain figures would suggest.

The engine was in the state of immaculate cleanliness that was characteristic of Stewarts Lane at that time. There was however a good deal more to it than mere spit and polish. She had amassed a total of 70,000 miles since last visit to plant for periodic overhaul, and yet had been so well maintained as to ride and work like a relatively new engine. There is no doubt that the Southern men took a great pride in the upkeep of their steam locomotives in the 1950s, though from statistics contained in a paper presented to the Institution of Locomotive Engineers in 1953 it would seem that the record of No 768 for mileage was passing above the average for the class. This was quoted for the entire King Arthur class as 70,995 miles. A friend who made some footplate journeys on No 768 some little time after my own, when she had amassed a mileage of 90,000, found her general working and detailed performance still quite undiminished in quality. Engine No 768 was indeed one of the most documented members of the entire class. She was chosen as representative of Stewarts Lane for the comparative coal trials of 1925-6, and many pages of Holcroft's book *Locomotive Adventure* are devoted to day to day details of her running between Victoria and Dover, and then between Waterloo and Salisbury. Then, after her transfer to the West of England, she made some of the most brilliant runs ever recorded between Salisbury and Exeter, as the logs in Chapter Five of that book bear witness.

Details of the outward run as far as Margate are shown in the accompanying log. This driver worked in the usual way, linking up to 15 per cent before easing the regulator back from the full open position; and despite her high mileage the engine ran very smoothly and quietly even when pulled up so far. The fast run from Bromley to Chatham was exhilarating on the footplate, especially when the engine was taken downhill to Farningham Road with the regulator wide open and 20 per cent cut-off, to reach 79mph very quickly. They were half expecting checks in the approach to Chatham, but they did not materialise, so that we arrived 3min early by the clock. From Sole Street, down the long bank,

3.35 p m VICTORIA-MARGATE
Load: 9 coaches, 301 tons tare, 315 tons full
Engine: 30768 Sir Balin
Driver: S. Gingell, Fireman: F.Rowe (Stewarts Lane)

Dist Miles		Sch. min.	Actual m s	Speeds m p h
0.0	VICTORIA	0	0 00	-
1.9	Wandsworth Road		5 15	-
4.0	HERNE HILL	8½	8 27	38
5.7	Sydenham Hill		11 37	28
8.7	BECKENHAM JUNC	16½	15 28	60
-			P W S	20
10.9	BROMLEY SOUTH	20	19 45	-
1.7	Bickley Junc	5	5 12	-
3.9	St. Mary Cray		7 55	65
6.8	SWANLEY JUNC	11	10 28	60
9.7	Farningham Road		13 09	79
12.6	Fawkham		15 27	69
15.0	Meopham		17 58	58/62
16.0	Sole Street	22	18 58	60
-	Cuxton Road		-	79
22.5	Rochester Junc	30½	26 20	-
23.4	CHATHAM	33	28 13	-
1.6	Gillingham		4 00	-
7.3	Newington		10 47	60/56
-			-	66
10.4	Sittingbourne	13	14 30	-
1.3	Milepost 46		2 47	58
3.3	Teynham		4 57	56/51½
-			-	64½
7.3	FAVERSHAM	11	9 47	-
3.0	Graveney Siding		4 46	61
7.1	WHITSTABLE	10	8 52	-
1.4	Chestfield	4	3 58	-
2.2	HERNE BAY	5	4 07	-
0.8	Milepost 63½		2 56	-
1.3	" 64		4 11	30
6.5	" 69½		9 32	74
8.0	Birchington	12	11 07	-
1.7	Westgate	4	4 36	-
1.5	MARGATE	4	3 36	-

Overall time from Victoria 132 min 50 sec

A potpourri at Basingstoke in 1954: two distinguished strangers, the GNR 4-4-2 No 251 and GCR 4-4-0 *Prince Albert* BR No 62663 with three King Arthurs: 30745 *Tintagel* back to the GCR engine; 30751 *Etarre* in the background, and 30780 *Sir Persant.*

Up relief West of England express approaching Semley in 1959: engine 30449 *Sir Torre.*

only the small valve of the regulator was used, with 15 per cent cut-off. From Chatham there was no time to spare anywhere. Between stations the engine was worked hard, with regulator full open and cut-off never less than 20 per cent. Out of Herne Bay, where the gradient is 1 in 101 for 1½ miles, the cut-off was 40 per cent from the start and up the bank, and then 20 per cent for the fast running on to Birchington. We arrived in Margate just ten seconds inside our overall allowance from Victoria.

From Margate I was invited to drive the engine—under appropriate supervision!—and following what I had seen the driver do from every stop so far, opened straight out to full regulator. There was no slipping, and on the steep rising gradients to Broadstairs, 1 in 80 at first, and then 1 in 110, I used 40 per cent cut-off. Concentrating on the engine controls I did no detailed timing, but I must have kept the point-to-point allowances for we were a minute early by the clock on arrival at Ramsgate, thus:—

Margate-Broadstairs, 3.2 miles, 8min
Broadstairs-Dumpton Park, 1.2 miles, 3min
Dumpton Park-Ramsgate, 1.0 miles, 3min
Sir Balin was a delightfully easy engine to handle, and I took her as far as Birchington on

9.25 p m   CHATHAM-BROMLEY SOUTH

Load: 9 coaches, 286 tons tare, 300 tons full

Engine: 30768 Sir Balin

Driver: S. Gingell, Fireman: F.Rowe (Stewarts Lane)

Dist		Sch	Actual		Speeds
Miles		min	m	s	m p h
0.0	CHATHAM	0	0	00	-
0.9	Rochester Bridge Jc	2½	2	02	-
3.4	Cuxton Road Box		7	25	35
7.4	Sole Street	15	15	00	31
8.4	Meopham		16	25	-
10.8	Fawkham		19	07	-
13.7	Farningham Road		21	29	86
16.6	SWANLEY JUNC	26	23	55	60
19.5	St. Mary Cray		26	37	69
-			sigs		5
21.7	Bickley Junc	32	30	57	-
23.4	BROMLEY SOUTH	35	34	25	-

Ramsgate express at St Mary Cray Junction in 1959: engine No 30799 *Sir Ironside.*

the return trip.

I have tabulated in detail only the express section, between Chatham and Bromley South. Mainly through slight overtime at stations we were 2½ min late from Chatham, and the driver was anxious to make up time, but our attack on the Sole Street was hindered a little at the start by the engine priming slightly. Above Cuxton Road, however, with full regulator and 45 per cent cut-off acceleration was strong, and downhill a maximum of no less than 86mph was attained in the dip at Farningham Road. This was the end of any spectacular running, because we were all but stopped by signals at St Mary Cray Junction, and were evidently following another train closely for the rest of the way into Victoria.

Throughout the Maunsell regime also the engine numbers were carried in large numerals on the tenders so that some renumbering of tenders was necessary to accord with their allocation to different locomotives. It was not until Bulleid's time that engine numbers were displayed in transfer numerals on the cabsides, and were removed entirely from the tenders. Apparently the combination of the Drummond tenders with the Urie-style cab on the G14

replacements created miniature dust storms, and Holcroft told me once how indescribably filthy he used to get when riding on those particular Arthurs. All my own footplate trips were made on engines fitted with Urie eight-wheeled tenders and were as clean and comfortable as one could expect on a steam locomotive. This brings me to the work of these engines in their last years, and just as their appearance remained unchanged so the work they were expected to do was little less than that required of them in the 1930s.

In the summer of 1954 I spent a day on engine No 30769 *Sir Balan,* on a round trip from Victoria to Dover Marine and back. The work demanded in hauling heavy Continental boat trains was no less, and no more than that when the Scotchmen were first put on to these trains and it was doubly interesting in that we went out via Maidstone, and returned via the old LC & D line via Canterbury and Chatham. I am dealing in some detail with the working, because in many ways it was quite an epitome of King Arthur performance. The engine was booked for a relief portion of the regular 10am Ostend-Brussels boat train and allowed 113min for the 81.1 miles from Victoria to Dover Marine. This involved a considerably slower average speed

One of the Urie S15s in BR days, with large diameter Maunsell chimney, and Drummond inside-framed 8-wheeled tender.

than that of the direct line trains, via Tonbridge, but the route includes many severe speed restrictions, in addition to heavy gradients.

The log on page 85 needs a good deal of further explanation. To Bickley Junction where we left the normal boat train route we had lost 5min by adverse signals, and we were then close on the tail of a local train until diverging from the Sevenoaks line at Otford. After that, apart from a permanent way check between Wrotham and Malling we had a clear road right through to the outskirts of Dover. The engine was strong at the front end and steaming perfectly, on hard coal, and between Otford and rejoining the main line at Ashford the gradients are very

awkward. At first it is a steeply graded switch-back, including adverse lengths of 1 in 82. The only appreciable length of favourable grade was spoiled for us by the permanent way check. Then after the sharp curve through Maidstone East comes the long ascent to Lenham, beginning with the vicious $1\frac{1}{2}$ miles at 1 in 60 up to Bearsted. The average inclination thence to the summit is about 1 in 150. Thence, although all downhill, this line is not suitable for much over 60mph and it concludes with a heavy slack joining the main line at Ashford.

The engine was worked with regulator fully opened on all the adverse lengths, and linked up to 17 per cent on easier stretches before any

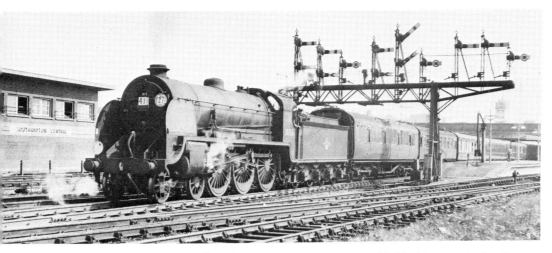

Bournemouth Express leaving Southampton with engine No 30763 *Sir Bors de Ganis.*

Up relief Bournemouth express at Worting Junction: engine No 30783 *Sir Gillemere.*

closing of the regulator took place. It was indeed quite a copy book performance. From Maidstone the cut-off was no less than 40 per cent up to Bearsted, and between 25 and 35 per cent on the easier continuation to Lenham. The driver was an artist with the reverser, making frequent adjustment to suit the constantly changing gradients. After Lenham he linked up to 17 per cent maintaining full regulator up to 60mph and then gradually easing back. It will be seen from the log that despite the permanent way check we had kept our point-to-point allowance from Otford B Junction to Ashford. Once on to the main line the engine was driven hard up to Westenhanger, sustaining 53-54mph on the 1 in 286 gradient, with 27 per cent cut-off throughout. After that we ran easily down to Dover. Our net time was about 4min inside schedule, and to

Margate express, diverted via Selling, because of flood damage: engine No 30768 *Sir Balin.*

One of the 1924-5 batch of H15s in BR days, No 30476, on Weymouth-Bournemouth local leaving Upwey Wishing Well Halt, in 1960.

9.40 a.m RELIEF CONTINENTAL BOAT EXPRESS
Load: 12 vehicles, 370 tons tare, 405 tons full
Engine: 30769 Sir Balan
Driver: P.Tutt, Fireman: R.Wilkes (Stewarts Lane)

Dist Miles		Sch min	Actual m s	Speeds m p h
0.0	VICTORIA	0	0 00	-
1.9	Wandsworth Road		4 30	34½
-			sigs	2
4.0	HERNE HILL	8½	9 20	
5.7	Sydenham Hill		14 02	25
8.7	BECKENHAM JUNC	16½	18 30	55
-			sigs	20
10.9	BROMLEY SOUTH		23 32	
12.6	Bickley Junc	23	28 00	
-			sigs	
14.8	St. Mary Cray		31 42	
-			sigs	
17.7	SWANLEY JUNC	29	36 05	
-			sig stop	
20.4	Evnsford		43 47	39/29
25.0	Otford 'B' Junc.	38	51 40	44
27.0	Kemsing		54 57	30½ (min)
29.6	Wrotham		58 51	53
-			p w s	15
34.7	Malling		65 34	66
37.5	Barming		68 17	56
39.9	MAIDSTONE EAST	60½	73 01	15*
42.7	Bearsted		79 06	30/18
45.0	Hollingbourne		82 59	39/28
47.4	Harrietsham		87 13	40½
49.1	Lenham		90 30	28
53.0	Charing		95 05	61
55.8	Hothfield		97 32	69
59.2	ASHFORD	88	101 44	slack
63.5	Smeeth		106 45	55½
67.3	Westenhanger		110 55	53
73.0	FOLKESTONE CEN	104	116 55	62 (max.)
74.0	Folkestone Junc		117 54	60
78.1	Shakespeare Box		122 55	-
-			sig stop	
82.0	DOVER MARINE	113	129 45	-

* Speed restriction

do this required about 45 gallons of water per mile. The coal consumption was probably around 60lb per mile, but on a journey with such intermittent demands for steam, and heavy spells, it was good work. The firing was most expertly done, with nothing wasted by blowing off.

At Dover the tender was topped up with soft, Kentish coal, and because of its slower burning quality a big fire was built up in readiness for the return journey. There were three trains in connection with the morning boat from Ostend; we had the second of the three, and in our 12 coaches it was estimated we had 1,000 passengers. Again with the line crowded with many trains there were numerous checks, and from the locomotive point of view the main interest lay in the climbing of the severe gradients: continuously 1 in 132 from Dover up to Shepherdswell, and from Canterbury up to Ensden Tunnel (milepost 56¼). Worst of all was the check to 5mph at Cuxton Road box of all places soon after the start of that severe five mile climb of Sole Street bank mostly at 1 in 100 out of the Medway valley. From the sustained speeds on these inclines I have made some estimates of

Up relief Continental Boat Express passing Bromley South: engine No 30769 *Sir Balan*
with the Author on the footplate.

the horsepower developed by this excellent
engine.

Location	Gradient 1 in	Speed mph	Cut-off per cent	Equiv. dbhp	ihp
Bearstead	60	18	40	1045	1090
Ensden Tunnel	132	34½	37	1065	1185
Westenhanger	286	53	27	1065	1340

The power developed in the climb out of Dover
was probably even higher than at Ensden
Tunnel, as the cut-off was 42 per cent and the
engine was still accelerating on the 1 in 132
gradient, having attained 33½ mph. Thus in the
year 1954 this engine was working up to the same
high standards of performance that had given
such satisfaction to the Southern Railway 29
years earlier.

The electrification of the Kentish main lines
sounded the death-knell of the King Arthur
class. Naturally the Urie N15s went first, and by
1958 all had been withdrawn. Then someone
had the curious idea of perpetuating their names
on some of the British Railways standard Class 5
mixed-traffic 4-6-0s. The 20 names originally
carried by engines 30736 to 30755 were
transferred though on *new* nameplates to
engines 73080-9 and 73110-9. The first of the

2.50 p m RELIEF CONTINENTAL BOAT EXPRESS
Load: 12 coaches, 389 tons tare, 425 tons full
Engine: 30769 Sir Balan
Driver: T. Tutt, Fireman: R.Wilkes (Stewarts Lane)

Dist Miles		Sch min	Actual m s	Speeds m p h
0.0	DOVER - Hawkesbury St	0*	0 00+	-
0.7	Dover Priory	4	3 07	-
2.9	Kearsney		9 28	30½
6.3	Shepherdswell		15 50	33½
10.2	Adisham		20 43	72½
-			sig stop	-
16.2	CANTERBURY	24	29 55	-
18.0	Milepost 60		33 16	34½
21.0	Milepost 57		38 30	34½
22.8	Selling		41 06	55½
24.0	FAVERSHAM	38	44 17	65
-			sigs	40
30.0	Teynham		49 03	54
33.3	SITTINGBOURNE	48	52 52	48½
35.0	Milepost 43		55 10	37
39.1	Rainham		60 09	54
43.7	CHATHAM	61	65 39	slack
46.0	Milepost 32		69 13	39
-			sigs	5
51.1	Sole Street	77	85 40	-
57.5	Farningham Road		93 08	71½
-			sigs	-
65.4	Bickley Junc	96	103 08	-
-			sigs	-
74.0	HERNE HILL	113	124 23	-
-			sig stop	-
78.0	VICTORIA	120	143 50	-

*   Schedule from Dover Marine
+   Times from restart at Hawkesbury St box

King Arthurs proper to be withdrawn was No
30454 *Queen Guinevere,* at the end of 1958.
After that the withdrawals were gradual and
spread over four years until, by the end of 1962
only one, No 30770 *Sir Prianius* remained in
traffic. The engine of the Salisbury-Waterloo

Up Bournemouth express near Brookwood: another 1960 picture: engine No 30773 *Sir Lavaine.*

record run, No 777 *Sir Lamiel* was set aside for preservation, and eventual display in the National Railway Museum. During the same period the H15s of both the 1913 and 1924 series were also withdrawn, the 482-491 batch having approached a life of 50 years.

There is a good story to be told about the last years of the King Arthurs. The Urie N15 *Merlin* was condemned, and some genius had the idea of sending the engine to her doom in spectacular fashion. She should be the victim of an act of sabotage. The line should be blown up at the moment she passed, and the event should be televised. I shall never forget that programme. The commentator drew a vivid picture of what was to happen: how the gallant old engine

would soon be reduced to a twisted heap of scrap iron, and as the regulator was opened and the crew jumped off *Merlin* was given a friendly pat of farewell. Then he fairly piled on the drama. 'You've never seen anything like it before' he yelled; and working up into that descriptive hysteria that is the acknowledged way of accompanying exciting events on the screen, he became almost inarticulate with frenzy as the engine approached the fatal spot. There was certainly an explosion, and *Merlin* was derailed; but she ran down one side of the shallow embankment, and stopped standing bolt upright and unscathed in a field, quietly blowing off as though ready to take the Atlantic Coast Express forward from Salisbury. I laughed my head off!

Up West of England express passing under the Battledown flyover with engine No 30450 *Sir Kay.*

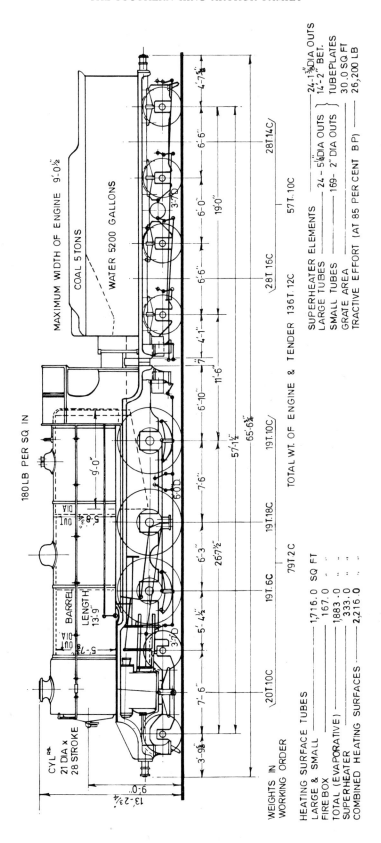

180 LB PER SQ IN

MAXIMUM WIDTH OF ENGINE 9'-0½"

COAL 5 TONS

WATER 5200 GALLONS

CYL RS
21 DIA x
28 STROKE

BARREL
LENGTH
13'-9"

9'-0"

13'-2¾"

9'-0"

WEIGHTS IN
WORKING ORDER

TOTAL WT. OF ENGINE & TENDER 136 T. 10 C

20 T. 10 C   19 T. 6 C   79 T. 2 C   19 T. 18 C   19 T. 10 C   28 T. 16 C   28 T. 14 C   57 T. 10 C

HEATING SURFACE TUBES
LARGE & SMALL .... 1,716.0 SQ FT
FIRE BOX .... 167.0 „ „
TOTAL (EVAPORATIVE) ..... 1,883.0 „ „
SUPERHEATER .... 333.0 „ „
COMBINED HEATING SURFACES ... 2,216.0 „ „

SUPERHEATER ELEMENTS ... 24 - 1⅜" DIA OUTS
LARGE TUBES .... 24 - 5¼" DIA OUTS } 14'-2" BET.
SMALL TUBES .... 169 - 2" DIA OUTS } TUBEPLATES
GRATE AREA .... 30.0 SQ FT
TRACTIVE EFFORT (AT 85 PER CENT BP) ... 26,200 LB

Line diagram and dimensions of Urie H15 4-6-0.

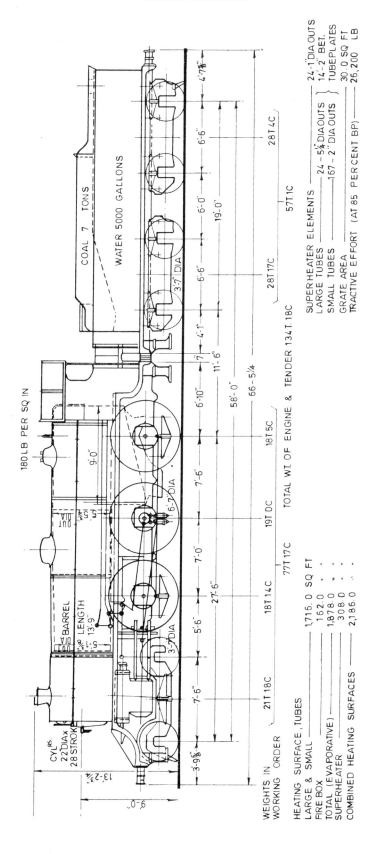

Line diagram and dimensions of Urie N15.

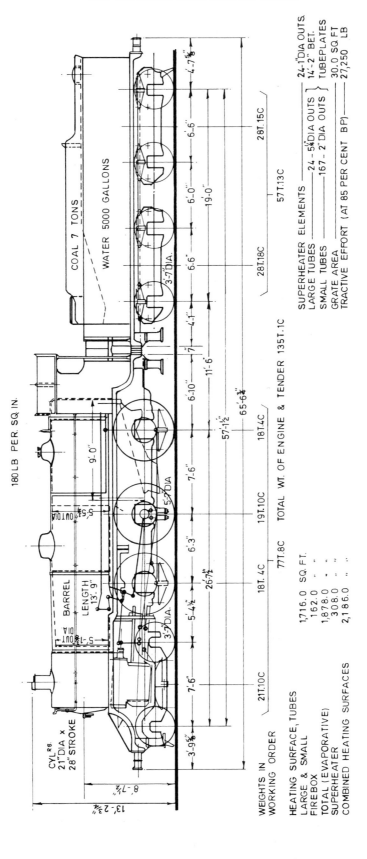

Line diagram and dimensions of Urie S15.

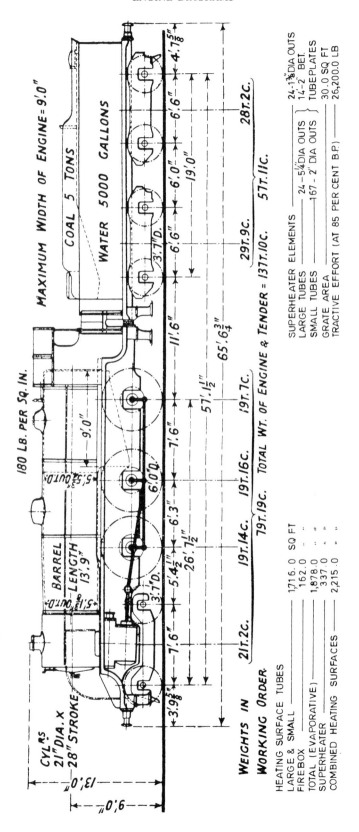

MAXIMUM WIDTH OF ENGINE = 9'0"

COAL 5 TONS

WATER 5000 GALLONS

180 LB. PER SQ. IN.

BARREL LENGTH 13'9"

CYL.RS 21" DIA. x 28" STROKE.

WEIGHTS IN WORKING ORDER.

21T.2C.	19T.14C.	19T.16C.	19T.7C.	28T.2C.

79T.19C. TOTAL WT. OF ENGINE & TENDER = 137T.10C.   57T.11C.

29T.9C.

HEATING SURFACE TUBES

LARGE & SMALL	1,716.0	SQ FT
FIREBOX	162.0	" "
TOTAL (EVAPORATIVE)	1,878.0	" "
SUPERHEATER	337.0	" "
COMBINED HEATING SURFACES	2,215.0	" "

SUPERHEATER ELEMENTS	24 - 1⅜"DIA OUTS		
LARGE TUBES	24 - 5¼"DIA OUTS	}	14'-2" BET. TUBEPLATES
SMALL TUBES	167 - 2" DIA OUTS		
GRATE AREA	30.0 SQ FT		
TRACTIVE EFFORT (AT 85 PER CENT B.P.)	26,200.0 LB		

Line diagram and dimensions of H15—1924 type.

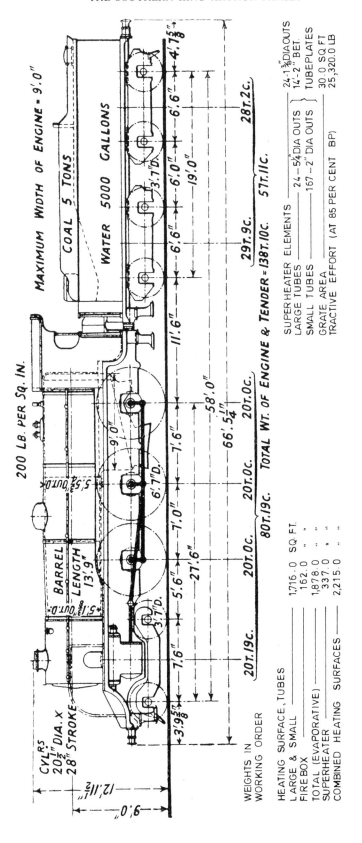

MAXIMUM WIDTH OF ENGINE = 9'.0"

COAL 5 TONS

WATER 5000 GALLONS

200 LB. PER SQ. IN.

CYL'RS
20½" DIA.X
28" STROKE

BARREL
LENGTH
13'.9"

TOTAL WT. OF ENGINE & TENDER = 138T.11C.

WEIGHTS IN
WORKING ORDER

HEATING SURFACE, TUBES
LARGE & SMALL ———————— 1,716.0 SQ. FT.
FIREBOX ————————————————— 162.0   "   "
TOTAL (EVAPORATIVE) ——————— 1,878.0   "   "
SUPERHEATER ———————————————— 337.0   "   "
COMBINED HEATING SURFACES ——— 2,215.0   "   "

SUPERHEATER ELEMENTS ——————— 24-1⅜"DIA OUTS
LARGE TUBES ——————— 24 - 5¼"DIA OUTS } 14'-2" BET.
SMALL TUBES ————————— 167 - 2" DIA OUTS } TUBEPLATES
GRATE AREA ——————————————————————— 30.0 SQ FT
TRACTIVE EFFORT (AT 85 PER CENT BP) ——— 25,320.0 LB

Line diagram and dimensions of King Arthur.

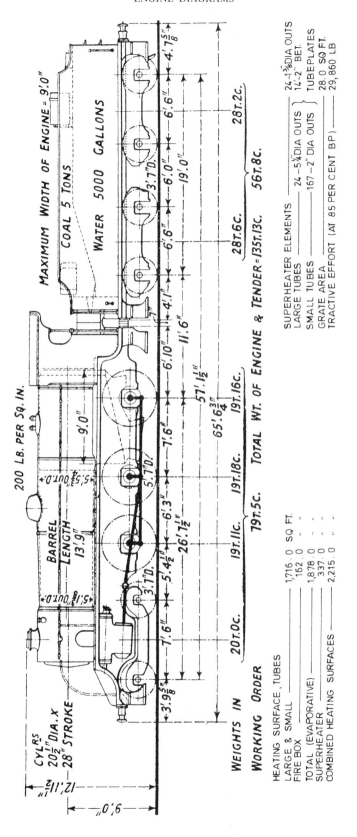

Line diagram and dimensions of Maunsell S15.

CASE HISTORIES

CLASS H15

(a) Urie (L S W R)

Engine No	Built	Maunsell Superheater	Withdrawn
482	2/14	10/34	5/59
483	3/14	9/29	6/57
484	4/14	1/31	5/59
485	6/14	9/28	4/55
486	12/13	3/30	7/59
487	1/14	5/29	11/57
488	3/14	3/28	4/59
489	5/14	3/32	1/61
490	6/14	5/29	6/55
491	7/14	6/27	2/61

(b) Rebuilds of Drummond 4-6-0s

330	10/24*		5/57
331	11/24*	When	3/61
332	11/24*	rebuilt	11/56
333	12/24*		10/58
334	1/25*		6/58
335	11/14*	12/27	6/59

(c) Built by Southern Railway

473	2/24	11/31	8/59
474	2/24	6/31	4/60
475	3/24	6/30	12/61
476	4/24	1/29	12/61
477	5/24	12/29	7/59
478	6/24	5/30	3/59
521	7/24	9/29	12/61
522	7/24	4/29	9/61
523	9/24	7/29	12/61
524	9/24	When built	2/61

* Dates of re-building

CLASS N15

(a) Urie (L S W R)

Engine No	Name	Built	Maunsell Superheater	Withdrawn
736	Excalibur	8/18	9/30	11/56
737	King Uther	10/18	6/29	6/56
738	King Pellinore	12/18	3/30	3/58
739	King Leodegrance	2/19	5/30	5/57
740	Merlin	3/19	12/29	12/55
741	Joyous Gard	5/19	2/28	2/56
742	Camelot	6/19	8/30	2/57
743	Lyonnesse	7/19	6/30	10/55
744	Maid of Astolat	9/19	1/30	1/56
745	Tintagel	11/19	12/31	2/56
746	Pendragon	6/22	1/29	10/55
747	Elaine	7/22	11/30	10/56
748	Vivien	8/22	11/29	9/57
749	Iseult	9/22	12/28	6/57
750	Morgan le Fay	10/22	2/30	7/57
751	Etarre	11/22	6/29	6/57
752	Linette	12/22	9/30	12/55
753	Melisande	1/23	7/28	3/57
754	The Green Knight	2/23	1/30	1/53
755	The Red Knight	3/23	3/29	5/57

(b) Replacements of Drummond G14 class

		Built	Withdrawn
448	Sir Tristram	5/25	8/60
449	Sir Torre	6/25	12/59
450	Sir Kay	6/25	9/60
451	Sir Lamorak	6/25	6/62
452	Sir Meliagrance	7/25	8/59
453	King Arthur	2/25	7/61
454	Queen Guinevere	3/25	11/58
455	Sir Lancelot	3/25	4/59
456	Sir Galahad	4/25	5/60
457	Sir Bedivere	4/25	5/61

(c) Buit by N B Loco Co Ltd (eight-wheeled tenders)

		Built	Withdrawn
763	Sir Bors de Ganis	5/25	10/60
764	Sir Gawain	5/25	7/61
765	Sir Gareth	5/25	9/62
766	Sir Geraint	5/25	12/58
767	Sir Valence	6/25	6/59
768	Sir Balin	6/25	10/61
769	Sir Balan	6/25	2/60
770	Sir Prianius	6/25	11/62
771	Sir Sagramore	6/25	3/61
772	Sir Percivale	6/25	9/61
773	Sir Lavaine	6/25	2/62
774	Sir Gaheris	6/25	1/60
775	Sir Agravaine	6/25	2/60
776	Sir Galagars	6/25	1/59
777	Sir Lamiel	6/25	10/61
778	Sir Pelleas	6/25	5/59
779	Sir Colgrevance	7/25	7/59
780	Sir Persant	7/25	7/59
781	Sir Aglovale	7/25	5/62
782	Sir Brian	7/25	9/62
783	Sir Gillemere	8/25	2/61
784	Sir Nerovens	8/25	10/59
785	Sir Mador de la Porte	8/25	10/59
786	Sir Lionel	8/25	8/59
787	Sir Menadeuke	9/25	2/59
788	Sir Urre of the Mount	9/25	2/62
789	Sir Guy	9/25	12/59
790	Sir Villiars	9/25	10/61
791	Sir Uwaine	9/25	5/60
792	Sir Hervis de Revel	10/25	2/59

(d) Built at Eastleigh for Central Section (six-wheeled tenders)

		Built	Withdrawn
793	Sir Ontzlake	3/26	8/62
794	Sir Ector de Maris	3/26	8/60
795	Sir Dinadan	4/26	7/62
796	Sir Dodinas le Savage	5/26	2/62
797	Sir Blamor de Ganis	6/26	6/59
798	Sir Hectimere	6/26	6/62
799	Sir Ironside	7/26	2/61
800	Sir Meleaus de Lile	9/26	8/61
801	Sir Meliot de Logres	10/26	4/59
802	Sir Durnore	10/26	7/61
803	Sir Harry le Fise Lake	11/26	8/61
804	Sir Cador of Cornwall	12/26	2/62
805	Sir Constantine	1/27	11/59
806	Sir Galleron	1/27	4/61

Note: the names of engines 736 to 755 were added from 1925 onwards

CLASS S15

(a) Urie (L S W R.)

Engine No	Date Built	Maunsell Superheater	Withdrawn
496	5/21	9/27	6/63
497	3/20	2/28	7/63
498	4/20	2/30	6/63
499	5/20	6/31	1/64
500	5/20	10/30	6/63
501	6/20	8/31	6/63
502	7/20	5/30	11/62
503	8/20	5/31	6/63
504	9/20	1/29	11/62
505	10/20	12/31	11/62
506	10/20	2/30	1/64
507	11/20	1/32	12/63
508	12/20	8/29	11/63
509	12/20	4/29	7/63
510	1/21	2/31	6/63
511	1/21	11/30	7/63
512	2/21	8/31	3/64
513	3/21	5/30	3/63
514	3/21	5/31	3/63
515	4/21	9/31	7/63

(b) Built by Southern Railway

Engine No	Date Built	Withdrawn
823	3/27	11/63
824	3/27	9/65
825	4/27	1/64
826	5/27	12/62
827	6/27	1/64

828	7/27		1/64
829	7/27		11/63
830	8/27		7/64
831	9/27		11/63
832	10/27		1/64
833	11/27		5/65
834	11/27		11/64
835	12/27		11/64
836	12/27		6/64
837	1/28		9/65

(b) Built by Southern Railway

Engine No	Date Built	Withdrawn
838	5/36	9/65
839	5/36	9/65
840	6/36	9/64
841	7/36	1/64
842	8/36	9/65
843	10/36	9/64
844	10/36	6/64
845	10/36	7/63
846	11/36	2/63
847	12/36	1/64

INDEX